Historical Research Using British Newspapers

Remembering my lovely grandparents
Mary and William Marshall
who fostered my love of reading

Historical Research Using British Newspapers

Denise Bates

PEN & SWORD
HISTORY

First published in Great Britain in 2016 by
Pen & Sword History
an imprint of
Pen & Sword Books Ltd
47 Church Street
Barnsley
South Yorkshire
S70 2AS

ISBN 978 1 47385 900 5

A CIP catalogue record for this book is available from the British
Library

Typeset in Ehrhardt by
Mac Style Ltd, Bridlington, East Yorkshire
Printed and bound in the UK by CPI Group (UK) Ltd,
Croydon, CRO 4YY

Pen & Sword Books Ltd incorporates the imprints of Pen & Sword
Archaeology, Atlas, Aviation, Battleground, Discovery, Family
History, History, Maritime, Military, Naval, Politics, Railways, Select,
Transport, True Crime, and Fiction, Frontline Books, Leo Cooper,
Praetorian Press, Seaforth Publishing and Wharncliffe.

For a complete list of Pen & Sword titles please contact
PEN & SWORD BOOKS LIMITED
47 Church Street, Barnsley, South Yorkshire, S70 2AS, England
E-mail: enquiries@pen-and-sword.co.uk
Website: www.pen-and-sword.co.uk

Contents

Introduction

The idea of writing a book about using old newspapers for historical research arose from the very positive reaction received to a blog I wrote for *The British Newspaper Archive*. My first two books, *Pit Lasses* and *Breach of Promise to Marry*, had each used on-line historical newspapers as a significant source of information. During the two periods of research, I not only gathered plenty of new information about my topics but also learned much about the practicalities of using on-line newspapers, a relatively new skill for a historian to master.

Translating this initial learning into a full length book has involved many more fascinating discoveries about three centuries of the British newspaper industry and how individual titles found their niche in the political, economic and social fabric of the country. It has been an exciting journey of discovery.

Although the name on the front cover is mine, researching and writing a book and steering the manuscript through the production process involves many more people than just the author. Four researchers, Rachel Bates, Angela Buckley, Suzie Grogan and Gill Hoffs have all used old newspapers in a different manner to my own and have generously written a short piece about their studies to help illustrate the innovative ways in which historians can approach this exciting source. Thanks are also due to commissioning editor Eloise Hansen and the production staff at Pen and Sword Books for all the practical tasks that contribute to turning a script into a newly printed book.

Pen and Sword are part of the same Ltd. group as the *Barnsley Chronicle*, a weekly newspaper that has served the town for over 150 years. Thanks are expressed to them for allowing me to use content from this newspaper for illustration. *The British Newspaper Archive* has generously allowed me to include material from its excellent collection and use screen shots from its on-line newspaper search facility. The help provided by Amy Sell and Megan Charnley at *The British Newspaper Archive* and by all the staff at the Barnsley Archive is greatly appreciated.

I believe that all the illustrative and example material I have included is either freely available or that I hold the necessary permission. All rights pertaining to any trade marks that may have been mentioned in the text are acknowledged. If anyone believes that I have infringed their rights, please contact me so that this can be corrected in any future editions.

Finally, I would like to thank my husband, sons, daughter-in-law, mother and mother-in-law for all the help, encouragement and practical support they have provided in their different ways. Without their valuable input this book would be the poorer.

Denise Bates
31st July 2015

Chapter 1

A Brief History of Newspapers in Britain

How the newspaper industry developed

Almost as soon as Johannes Gutenberg developed his revolutionary mechanical printing equipment in the mid-fifteenth century, news sheets, pamphlets and posters flew off the new-style presses. Up-to-date commercial information had a ready audience amongst a growing entrepreneurial class of traders, merchants and brokers and the *London Gazette* – founded in 1665 as the *Oxford Gazette* – is usually regarded as Britain's first newspaper.

Commercial news and studies of weighty subjects were the respectable element of this early publishing industry and gradually evolved into reputable newspapers and periodicals. Other printed matter was more brash and brazen. Openly poking fun, challenging authority and disseminating scandal, it appealed to the baser instincts of human nature.

By the early decades of the eighteenth century, more than a dozen publications were in existence covering many types of news but their development was rued by the ruling classes and successive governments tried to suppress the flow of knowledge to the wider populace. One tactic was to restrict what could be circulated in print. Reporting anything about the business or apparatus of government, even if the story was truthful, or advocating change against the wishes of the ruling elite, was to court trouble. Harsh measures were taken against subversives who published unwelcome details and editors and writers could easily find themselves in court charged with seditious libel. This was a very serious crime which involved bringing into disrepute the public institutions of the country, such as Parliament, the monarchy and the legal system and those involved in running them. A guilty verdict usually meant punitive fines or jail, which effectively meant the end for the newspaper as it had been deprived of its money or its editor, or both.

A less draconian tactic was to tax every copy of a newspaper that was sold. This artificially raised its price, keeping those on small incomes out of the market but enabling the thriving commercial class to obtain information that was relevant for their business. This tax, known as Stamp Duty, was first imposed in 1712 but the low rate of a halfpenny (½d) per copy was not excessive. In 1797, as Britain's ruling class shuddered at the thought of the French Revolution triggering a similar uprising by the British poor, Stamp Duty was increased to 3½d to try to suppress news about events across the Channel. The defeat of Napoleon Bonaparte in 1815 failed to diminish upper class anxiety about a revolt amongst British workers and, in response to industrial unrest, Stamp Duty was raised to 4d, perhaps more than half the cost of the paper. By 1819, workers' unrest had intensified and further measures were brought in to try to stifle dissent. More publications were brought within the scope of Stamp Duty and publishers had to enter into bonds and lodge money with the authorities to guarantee that they would only print what was lawful.

In the 1830s the official mood was more benign. The spectre of imminent revolution by the poor had ceased to haunt the ruling classes and some recognised that good newspaper editors were working to high professional standards. By 1836, Stamp Duty had been reduced to 1d as those who exercised political power began to realise how well their own interests might be served by informed public opinion. In 1843, Lord Campbell steered a Libel Act through Parliament. This made it easier for newspapers to report what was happening as editors could now defend themselves in criminal proceedings by demonstrating that the statement complained of was true and that printing it was for the public benefit. In 1855, during a period of relative social calm and economic prosperity, but also a time of war in the Crimean Peninsula, Stamp Duty on newspapers was abolished completely in Britain. After more than 150 years of official repression and obstruction, newspapers and their editors were at liberty to publish the truth, to highlight unfairness and to campaign for reform as they chose.

Key National Developments

Despite the background of suppression, the growing middle-class maintained a lively interest in keeping abreast of what was new and from the mid–eighteenth century onwards, a variety of national, provincial and local papers began to find

A Printing Press.
(*Author's Collection*)

readers who were keen to know what was being discussed in Parliament. The first national newspapers to develop into regular publications were established around 1770, the time when political parties with distinctive views were beginning to form. Although the ruling elite normally regard the general dissemination of news as undesirable, a contradictory factor was now at work: the need to keep people of the same political opinions up-to-date. Influencers were aware that news sheets could play an important role in this and, on occasions, formed links with a sympathetic editor to get their messages out to the literate public. This probably explains why, in a repressive climate, some newspapers managed to establish themselves and become regarded as respectable.

Most eighteenth century newspapers began as irregular publications, starting out as a large sheet or two that was printed once, or perhaps twice, a week when there enough new material to fill the page. Of all the titles published, only a few prospered. Many survived for just a short period, mainly because they did not make money for their owner. Some were set up to campaign on a particular topic and faded away or amalgamated with another paper if their objective was achieved or became irrelevant. Others depended upon the drive and commitment of a key individual for getting each edition to press and struggled as soon as that person was no longer involved. Amongst all the national papers that were printed, a few stand out for their high quality reporting or because they appealed to a wide section of the populace. These are likely to be used extensively be researchers.

The Morning Chronicle

The Morning Chronicle was founded in 1769, and gradually became associated with the Whig Party, a progressive group that was most likely to listen favourably to calls for political or social reform. It provides valuable insight into the practicalities of disseminating news stories and advocating change in the late-eighteenth and early-nineteenth centuries. In the mid-nineteenth century when official attitudes had become more relaxed it employed some notable, reformist contributors including the writer Charles Dickens and political philosopher John Stuart Mill. It also commissioned some very authoritative studies into what life was really like for the poor. After Stamp Duty on newspapers was abolished in 1855, newspapers that catered for a range of tastes and interests developed and probably drew some readers away. The final edition of the *Morning Chronicle* was published in 1865, though its publication had been intermittent for a couple of years before that.

The Morning Post

The Morning Post was first published in 1772. Initially, it was supportive of the emerging Whig Party but within a generation it was promoting moderate Tory views. In the early-nineteenth century it was a rival to the more progressive *Morning Chronicle*, attracting contributors such as William Wordsworth and Charles Lamb. After 1855, *The Morning Post* adapted successfully to the more crowded market-place, establishing itself as a supporter of conservatism in public life. It continued to publish until 1937 when it was taken over by the *Daily Telegraph*, which was serving the same readership.

The Times

The Times was founded in 1785, as the *Universal Daily Register,* by John Walter to advertise a new printing system for which he held the patent. It changed its name in 1788. Initially a four page newspaper, it carried a mixture of advertising, commercial, political and military news and notices and some reports from the law courts.

The Times developed its formidable reputation for quality journalism in the first half of the nineteenth century under editors Thomas Barnes (1817-41) and his successor John Delane (1841-77). The two men believed that a newspaper should be free both to report the truth and to comment on it. As official attitudes became more tolerant these editors did so on many occasions, earning *The Times* the reputation of being Britain's most influential newspaper and its nickname, *The Thunderer*.

The Times is regarded as the newspaper of record and is an indispensable source when researching major national events and issues of social concern, though it should never be treated uncritically. Although it has usually maintained an independent stance rather than taking a political line, it was less likely to champion change than some other publications and there are periods when it seems to be promoting an official viewpoint rather than providing a truly independent analysis. There are also instances where the newspaper had formed a firm opinion and where the coverage may have been designed to steer readers towards this view rather than representing the actual position.

The Guardian

Several regions of the country had a serious newspaper that concentrated on economic and social issues in the area's largest town and its hinterland. *The Manchester Guardian* was the one which made the transition from a provincial to a national English newspaper. It was established as a weekly publication in 1821 and began to publish daily in 1855 after the removal of Stamp Duty. It changed its name to *The Guardian* in 1959 and only moved from its Manchester roots to London in the 1960s.

The Manchester Guardian developed as a newspaper of significance under the long editorship of Charles Prestwich Scott (1871-1928) who demanded high quality writing, accuracy in reporting and a balanced approach, believing that 'comment is free but the facts are sacred'. During his editorship the paper stepped into the reformist void left by *The Morning Chronicle* when it ceased publication in 1865. Unlike other national newspapers which tended to promote the status quo, *The Guardian* was prepared to discuss unpopular or controversial causes, present minority views and report dissent.

The Guardian is an excellent resource for researchers for two reasons. Its willingness to reflect anti-establishment attitudes shows that society was often much less unified than other newspapers may indicate. It is also a very good place to find material relating to the north of England, an important industrial area in the nineteenth and twentieth centuries.

The Daily Telegraph

The Daily Telegraph was first published in 1855 as *The Daily Telegraph and Courier*. Although it positioned itself as a reformist publication, it differed from other national newspapers in that politics and reform was not one of its main interests. It covered political news but included other unrelated subjects such as science, business and fashion. It also carved out a niche promoting and sometimes raising funds for public and charitable causes.

The success of *The Daily Telegraph and Courier* in establishing itself in a competitive market demonstrates that politics was not an all-consuming passion of the literate public, even those who were politically aware. It perhaps explains why the more campaigning *Morning Chronicle* began to struggle when readers had a greater choice of newspaper content.

In 1937, *The Daily Telegraph* bought one of its competitors for the same market share, *The Morning Post*. The resultant publication was the conservatively-minded *Daily Telegraph*.

Technical and Social Developments

Although the reduction of Stamp Duty was important to the development of printed news, it was just one of several factors that helped British newspapers grow from a few weekly or bi-weekly publications, which targeted a narrow section of society, into daily editions, produced on an industrial scale and catering for a diverse and voracious readership. By 1840, a combination of increased scientific knowledge and the ability to translate this new understanding into practical applications, had speeded up the news-gathering, printing and distribution processes.

Until the development of the electric telegraph system in the 1830s, journalists had to deliver their copy to an editor via a slow and unreliable postal system. Stories could take several days to make their way into print, perhaps even after a rival newspaper had already broken the news. As telegraph offices began to open in large and small towns throughout the country, reporters could have their material transmitted back to the office within hours, giving editors of successful papers enough news to justify printing daily editions of their paper. Around the same time, the postal service became more regular and reliable, allowing reports and sketches to be posted to a newspaper office with confidence that delivery would be speedy.

By the mid-nineteenth century, production technology was innovating rapidly. Simultaneous printing on both sides of a sheet of paper, automatic paper feeds from large rolls, machine cutting and automatic folding of pages all became the norm, enabling newspapers to be produced quickly and in quantity. The machinery that made all this possible demanded a substantial amount of capital and newspaper proprietors who made a heavy investment in plant and premises wanted to recoup their outlay as quickly as possible rather than have expensive equipment standing idle. Speedy distribution of each edition across the country became ever more practical as the new railway network linked cities, towns and villages together. All of these technical developments cumulatively made daily editions of popular newspapers a sound business proposition.

Meanwhile, the number of customers was growing by the decade. By the time Stamp Duty was finally abolished, Britain had shaken off the privations of the 'hungry forties', a decade of severe economic hardship, and was entering a period of prosperity. Better understanding of how diseases spread resulted in sanitary reforms which gradually produced longer life-expectancy. A gradual reduction in child mortality, initially amongst the better-off, but eventually across all classes, also contributed to a noticeable increase in the population.

A prospering economy meant that new business opportunities opened up a range of technical, office and shop-based roles and a supply of literate workers was needed to fill them. In 1870, elementary education became compulsory for all children which, over a few decades, led to increased literacy amongst adults from the less affluent classes. By the 1880s, advances in shipping and refrigeration enabled Britain's wholesalers to import cheap food in bulk from around the world. Prices in the shops began to fall, which meant that the weekly wage stretched further and gave even manual workers a little discretionary spending power. All of this created the conditions for the further expansion of the newspaper industry.

Mass Market Newspapers

As the nineteenth century drew to a close, there was a readership whose needs were not being catered for by the established daily newspapers. Lower-middle class and working class people did not always have strong enough reading skills to cope with long articles or complex language, especially if they only had a small amount of free time. Many of them were not interested in the subjects that enthused their social betters; detailed information about politics, the Empire, world trade or the royal family had much less relevance to their daily lives.

The *Daily Mail, Daily Express* and *The Daily Mirror* were founded in 1896, 1900 and 1903 respectively. Although the Prime Minister, Lord Salisbury, dismissed the *Daily Mail* as being 'written by office boys for office boys' it cost just one halfpenny, half the price of many other papers and substantially less than *The Times* at 3d. The new titles quickly found an audience with the lower-middle classes who appreciated their brash mix of news and entertainment.

Despite appealing to the less affluent, the new mass-market titles were largely supportive of the established social order. They did not challenge the status quo or promote the concerns of the working man or woman. The *Daily Herald* and the *Daily Citizen* both came to market in 1912, a time of serious industrial unrest, to voice the worker's point of view. The *Daily Citizen* was a short-lived publication but the *Daily Herald* resonated with working class readers and survived until 1964 when it was relaunched as *The Sun*. This was the last major newspaper to be established until 1986, when the *Independent* was launched.

Weekly Newspapers

Alongside the papers that published an edition from Monday to Saturday, others elected to bring out just one edition each week. Amongst these were *The Observer, The Illustrated London News, News of the World, Lloyds, Reynolds* and *The Illustrated Police News*. These papers were often published on Sunday, when the dailies did not produce an edition, enabling them to garner an audience on a day when there was no competition from a reader's daily paper. They also

Newspaper Advertising Sign.
(*Author's Collection*)

attracted custom from people who had only the time, money or interest to read one paper a week and allowed printers to maximise the productivity of their equipment.

The weekly publication had a different approach to daily ones. With the exception of *The Observer* which was founded in the late-eighteenth century, most of the successful Sunday newspapers were established in the 1840s. By this time, wily proprietors understood why customers chose one paper instead of another. Sensation and scandal were key selling points, even amongst those who would have considered themselves above such conduct, and illustrations were also very well-received, perhaps an indication that densely packed pages of tiny print are not appealing to many readers.

Newspapers which published once each week were well-placed to supply an audience with the titillation it craved. They had seven days to source the most salacious stories from across the country or across the world and to commission illustrations. Although it may seem that scandal abounded in Victorian Britain, all the Sunday papers regularly included the same stories. It is unlikely that a daily paper, reporting in a similar vein, could have sustained such a high level of sensational content for six editions a week. Whilst their success proves there was a widespread demand for vicarious thrills across all levels of society, drawing wider lessons from them is unwise. Much of their content focussed on atypical happenings.

Weekly newspapers of all types are a useful starting point for research. They may be the most detailed record available for a sensational item, as respectable daily papers were sometimes circumspect about printing too much scandalous copy. For news that developed over two or more days

Newspaper Advertising Sign.
(*Author's Collection*)

they present the salient points in a single report, enabling a reader to get a quick grasp of a story. They are also a good source for illustrations.

Provincial and Local Newspapers

Complementing, and to some extent competing with, the national publications was a vast network of regional, county, town and even locality newspapers that began to develop in the early-eighteenth century and survived well into the twentieth. Some regional papers, including the *Norfolk Chronicle,* had their county name in their title, others such as *The Leeds Intelligencer* and *The York Herald* took the name of a city or town but their content had a much wider remit than just this stated area. Some of these newspapers eventually extended their remit and title. *The Leeds Intelligencer* became *The Yorkshire Post,* absorbed other papers from Leeds and Yorkshire and developed into a county-wide paper rather than one serving just West Yorkshire. A similar process took place in Scotland whereby some of its regional papers developed a pan-country focus.

The initial success of provincial newspapers reflected their practical role in disseminating the news from around the country before the railways developed. What distinguished provincial papers from titles that tried to serve the whole country, was the amount of material sourced from the area where the paper was produced. Additionally most regional papers, and those serving large towns, carried a substantial amount of information about British politics, law and the armed forces along with happenings around the world and stories from other regions, that may have been copied verbatim from another publication.

This meant that provincial newspapers were usually outward looking and papers that served distant places such as Orkney or Cornwall included plenty of news from across the British Isles and the wider world. Daily life in some of these remote communities in the nineteenth century would have been very different to life in the commercial centres and major industrial towns, but people who lived in them would have been well-informed about political events and technical progress if they could read.

As the nineteenth century progressed, many towns had at least one paper and often two or more. Sometimes they were printed by rival publishers and sometimes the same publisher produced both a morning and an evening paper. Stories included in an evening paper would often feature in the morning edition the following day. Small towns, and districts of a larger town, may have had their own local papers because some publishers produced separate titles for several places in the same area. Most of their content was standard across all the papers, with identical coverage of national or regional stories and the same specialist features, but a small section of paper was allocated to very local news.

A perennial problem for local newspapers is that, compared to national ones, their potential market is small. Local newspapers were businesses which had to make a profit if they were to survive. This meant attracting both advertisers and readers. Some struggled to find a market and quickly folded, especially if another paper was vying for the same custom. Competition was not always healthy and, on occasions, it was the last paper still being published rather than the best one that became a feature of local life. In some places, one or more titles amalgamated to create a viable paper. In others, the publisher recognised that there was neither market nor content enough for a daily paper and built up a business by printing weekly instead.

During the twentieth century, the content of local newspapers became much more focussed on their own area. The expansion of national daily newspapers, later followed by radio and television news broadcasts, meant that readers no longer needed national news from their local paper. What type of paper a household read was a matter of personal choice, if they could only afford one. Some preferred the national news whilst others chose the local. In areas that were more distant from London, many people saw local news as more relevant than what was happening in the wider world. This may have meant that people in the provinces were less aware of national issues than they would have been a few decades earlier if they read only a local paper and did not have a wireless.

However small or large their area of circulation, regional and local newspapers are an excellent resource for a historian as they contain detailed information about how an area developed and reveal how national developments affected specific parts of the country.

Specialist Newspapers

As well as papers that could appeal to any reader, plenty had a target readership in mind. They could be a tool for conducting a campaign for change, or serving an interest group that needed a certain type of news. Agriculture, then a key industry, had its own specialist publications throughout the nineteenth century. For much of the twentieth century, Sheffield printed the *Green Un* on Saturday evenings, devoted to local sport. Although financial newspapers managed to publish daily, many specialist publications only published weekly as there was not enough topic-based news to report.

Magazines and Periodicals

Many titles which provided information and news about special interests, or for an identified type of reader, developed as magazines or periodicals rather than as newspapers. In format they were smaller in size, easier to handle and illustrate, and potentially more durable. *The Gentleman's Magazine*, first published in 1731 and surviving into the twentieth century, is regarded as the first publication of this type, bringing together information on a number of topics that might interest an educated reader. The shorter-lived *Lady's Magazine* followed in 1770.

The terms magazine and periodical were initially interchangeable. Over time, 'magazine' came to denote a collection of material that was written at a level many readers could understand, whilst periodical acquired a more scholarly overtone.

Despite the difference in format there was not a rigid distinction of content between newspapers and magazines. Newspapers regularly published detailed articles and advice on interests such as transport and fashion. Magazines regularly included features about newsworthy topics or authoritative pieces of commentary about new developments. A historian who is researching a topic will find relevant material in both types of publication.

The Relevance of Historical Newspapers

Millions of newspaper pages have survived in archives, either in their original form or on microfilm. The practicalities of accessing them means that users have tended to be professional researchers or academics. In the last few years, an increasing number of newspapers have been digitised and made available on-line to anyone interested, at times and places which are convenient to the user rather than the institution that houses them. A new resource of such unprecedented scale and variety is certain to provide new and surprising insights, particularly into social history. Unlocking knowledge from this rich, but potentially unwieldy, source requires some specific skills. As well as knowing what titles are available, researchers need to appreciate how the media industry operated, the different types of material that can be found in newspapers, and the strengths and limitations of this source. They also need to know how to locate and evaluate relevant information and draw out informed, evidence-based conclusions. It promises to be the start of an exciting new phase in historical investigation and one that, thanks to digitisation, is equally open to professional and amateur researchers.

Chapter 2

The News Chain

Circulated on material that lacks durability and soon superseded by the next edition, the survival of so many old newspapers from as early as the seventeenth century is, at first glance, surprising. A piece of extraordinary foresight, otherwise known as Legal Deposit, accounts for this. From 1662, publishers have been obliged to place a copy of everything they printed with the country's copyright libraries. In a time of scientific discovery, the intention was to build repositories of knowledge on any topic and the obligation extended to flimsy and ephemeral products with a short life such as newspapers as well as to lavishly bound books. The legacy for the modern historian is the capture of some material which would never have been recorded in any other form. The extraordinary and varied amount of detail that has been preserved in newspapers makes it possible to establish how people lived in the past and what were the matters that concerned them, on a weekly, if not daily, basis.

There was no unique method of setting up a newspaper. The canny owner of a printing press may have used its spare capacity to generate extra income or advertise his services by issuing a news sheet. Someone with money and a story to peddle might have paid for a news sheet to be printed. Whether this translated into a viable newspaper was a matter of luck. A wide skill set that included commercial acumen, contacts who could provide a steady stream of new content, proficiency in writing and editing, the ability to use technical equipment and a distribution network were all essential. A source of capital to defray upfront costs such as printing or an editor's time was also necessary.

Proprietors

Capital and commercial acumen were provided by a newspaper's owners, often known as proprietors. Other than in the seventeenth and eighteenth centuries, when a few enterprising individuals tried to make their fortune by collecting

The Leeds Intelligencer.

Printed by THOMAS WRIGHT, at NEW-STREET END.

[Price THREE-PENCE.] TUESDAY, *February* 13, 1787. [Vol. XXXIII. Nº. 1698.]

MASQUERADE.

On Wednesday Evening, the 14th of February, 1787,

(By PERMISSION,)

WILL be a GRAND MASQUERADE, under the Management of Capt. PRIESTLEY, in the Great Room at the Rose-and-Crown Inn, Leeds.

Captain PRIESTLEY begs Leave to Apologize to the Ladies and Gentlemen for his altering the Day which was before fixed, has he did not at that Time recollect, the 25th Inst. will be the first Day in Lent.

Admission Tickets 3s. 6d. each, which Tickets will admit two Ladies, or one Gentleman and Lady.

Capt. PRIESTLEY will thank those Ladies and Gentlemen who mean to honour him with their Company, to apply for Tickets on or before the 8th of February; and at the same Time wishes to inform them, that they will not be desired to unmasque during the Course of the Entertainment.

In an adjoining Room will be a Cold Collation, gratis.

Masques may be had of Mr. Reynolds, Hardwareman, the Corner of Boar-Lane.

The Masquerade will open at Ten o'Clock precisely.

☞ Tickets to be had at the Printing-Office.

Mercery and Woollendrapery Goods.

Now Selling Off, at Prime Cost,

Opposite COWLING's HOTEL, Briggate, LEEDS,

ALL the STOCK IN TRADE of Mr EDWARD SANDERSON, Mercer and Woollen Draper, declining Business, consisting of Half Ell and Three-quarters Wide plain, striped and figured SILKS, which will be sold very low.

Also, Superfine Cloths, Plains, Hunters and Coatings, Silk and Stuffs, Corduroys, Thicksets and Fustians, Black Silks, Sattins, Modes and Persians, Bombazeens and Crapes, Wildbores and Tammies, Callimancos, Shalloons, Flannels, and all Kinds of Trimmings, Superfine Cloths of the best Fabric, at 16s. and 17s. per Yard, and all other Articles proportionably low.

NOW SELLING OFF

At PRIME COST, and UNDER,

ALL the STOCK IN TRADE, of Mr. JOSEPH ROSS, Linen-Draper and Haberdasher, in the Market-Place, LEEDS, (who is going to reside in the City of Glasgow) consisting of a large and fashionable Assortment of every Article in the above Branches, particularly a very valuable Collection of Muslins, Irish Linens, and Scots Hollands, and a numerous Assortment of Printed Goods of every Denomination; and as an Advance of full 6d. per Yard has taken Place on Prints, and most other Articles in the Cotton Trade, the Public will find their Advantage in embracing this Opportunity.

NOTICE to CREDITORS.

ALL Persons to whom GEORGE PEELE, late of Leeds, Taylor, deceased, stood indebted at the Time of his Decease, are desired to send an Account of their Demands to Mr. William Fotherby, of Leeds, Cloth-dresser, or Mr. Christopher Fotherby, of the same Place, Executors of the last Will and Testament, of the said George Peele or to Mr. Johnson, of Leeds, Attorney at Law, in order that the same may be discharged; and all Persons who stood indebted to the said George Peele, at the Time of his Decease, are desired to pay their respective Debts to the said Executors, or Mr. Johnson.

CREDITORS.

THE Commissioners in a Commission of Bankrupt, awarded and issued against WILLIAM JOHNSON, now or late of Halifax, in the County of York, Dyer, Dealer and Chapman, intend to meet on Saturday the Third Day of March next, at Ten in the Morning, at the House of Mrs. Lydia Newton, the Cross-Pipes in Halifax aforesaid, in order to make a Dividend of the said Bankrupt's Estate and Effects; when and where the Creditors who have not already proved their Debts, are to come prepared to prove the same, or they will be excluded the Benefit of the said Dividend: And all Claims not then proved will be disallowed.

☞ The Dividends will not be paid at the Time and Place abovementioned, but on any Saturday following, at the White-Swan in Halifax.

WAKEFIELD, 2d February, 1787.

IT appearing to us that there are several Abuses in the Paper Circulation of this Country, we the under-written do request a Meeting of the Gentlemen, Merchants and others, of the West Riding of Yorkshire, to be held at the White Hart, in Wakefield, on Thursday the 22d Instant, at Eleven o'Clock in the Forenoon, to take the same into Consideration:

Jo. Walker	W. Royston
B. Frank	M. Darbyshire
William Beatson	William White
P. Milnes	William Ottley
W. Dawson	John Naylor
Samuel Tooker	Thomas Hewitt
John Blayds	George Oddy
James Wilkinson	Richard Ambler
H. Zouch	Joseph Scarth
Thomas Rayner	Harper Soulby
Francis Edmunds	Thomas Clarkson
Joshua Wilson	William Bayley
Henry Wood	John Horsfall
Robert Lumb	John Drake
Samuel Lumb	William Lawton
John Lumb	Benjamin Mitchell
Thomas Lumb	Ed. Elwick and Son
James Milnes	William Skurray
James Milnes, Jun.	Thomas Hardy, Jun.
William Denton	George Brooke
John Clarke	William Shackleton
Jo. Hargreave	Thomas Smith.
John Earnshaw	

WEST-RIDING of YORKSHIRE.

AT the General Quarter Sessions held at Doncaster, in and for the said Riding, it appeared to the Court, That a large Quantity of PROMISSORY NOTES, payable to Bearer, a Number of Days after Sight in London, being now in Circulation, and continually encreasing, to the great Inconvenience of Trade: the Grand Jury, with the Concurrence and Approbation of the Bench of Justices at the Quarter Sessions held at Doncaster the 17th of January, 1787, have unanimously come to a Resolution not to take any more of them in Payment, they therefore recommend it to the People in general to be cautious of taking any in future.

James Backhouse, Darlington,	31	Days after Sight in London.
Richardson and Mawbrey, Darlington,	31	Ditto.
Lumley, Brown and Co. Stockton,	31	Ditto.
Tees Bank,	31	Ditto.
Whitehaven,	40	Ditto.
Mosney,	35	Ditto.
Lynn,	31	Ditto.
Wakefield,	31	Ditto.

Approved of by the Grand Jury, Doncaster Session., 1787.

THOMAS PARKER, Foreman.

Ordered by the Court to be advertised, with their fullest Approbation and Recommendation, in the York, Sheffield, Doncaster, and Leeds Papers.

EFFINGHAM, Chairman.

N. B. *The Public is requested to take Notice*, That the foregoing Banks were such as immediately occurred to the Grand Jury at the Time; but that this their Resolution was meant to extend to all other Banks, and Individual Persons, issuing Bills or Notes in the same Manner.

A CAUTION.

WHEREAS a Person assuming the different Names of JAMES WALKER, JAMES POPPLEWELL, &c. &c. has frequently in the Course of the two last Years, defrauded several Persons at York, Knaresborough, and other Places, of various Sums of Money, sometimes pretending he is an intimate Acquaintance, at others, that he is the Brother of the Rev. Mr. WALKER, of Northowram, near Halifax, whose Friends they are to whom he chiefly applies, saying that he is a Shalloon or Tammy-Maker, and that he is collecting his Debts, but being disappointed of receiving them, solicits the Loan of a little Money, in which he has often succeeded.

☞ Mr. Walker therefore thinks it necessary to caution the Public against the said Impostor.

A BOOK-KEEPER.

WANTED, A BOOK-KEEPER, that understands Italian—or more agreeable if Italian and French.——A satisfactory Recommendation will be expected.

☞ Enquire of Thomas Wright, Printer, Leeds.

WATER-MILLS.

WANTED, A MILL, with a constant and regular Supply of Water, near a Town or Village where a Number of Children may be had on easy Terms.

☞ A Situation in Derbyshire, or the East-Riding of Yorkshire, would be preferred.

Apply by Letter Post paid, to Mr John Gore, Liverpool.

To BRICK MAKERS.

WANTED Immediately, a NUMBER of WORKMEN to make BRICKS in the BOGGARD CLOSES, in Leeds.

Apply to Mr. Abraham Croft, Joiner; Mr. George Smith, in Kirkgate; or Mr. Johnson, Attorney at Law, all in Leeds.

SERVANT WANTED.

WANTED Immediately, a Middle-aged Man, to serve in the Capacity of FOOTMAN, in a regular Family in the Country. He must produce an undeniable Character for Honesty, Sobriety, and Integrity.

☞ Apply to the Printer of this Paper. No Letters answered unless Post-paid.

LEEDS, December 23, 1786.

I Do hereby caution the Public against an Advertisement inserted in this Paper of the 19th of December Inst. for SALE of several FREEHOLD ESTATES, in such Advertisement, said to be late of Mr. JOHN FENNEY, to enquire of Mr. Robert Priestley, Surgeon, in Leeds: *And this is to inform them*, That the said Advertisement is spurious and malicious.

JOHN FENNEY.

COOPERS' CREDITORS.

NOTICE is hereby given, to the Creditors of JAMES COOPER, of Leeds, and JOHN COOPER, of London, that have executed the Deed of Assignment made for the Benefit of their Creditors, That a Final Dividend of the Money, arising from the Sale of their Estate and Effects, will be paid by Messrs. John and George Shaw, of Leeds, on Saturday the 24th Day of February Inst. or any Day afterwards, at their Accompting House.

To be LETT, to enter to immediately,

Situate at Little-Woodhouse, near Leeds,

A Good New-built DWELLING-HOUSE, fitting for a genteel Family.

☞ For Particulars enquire of Mr. Samuel Park, in Lower-head-Row, Leeds, the Owner.

To be LETT,

TO ENTER TO IMMEDIATELY,

AN ESTATE called CLOSES, situate in LIVERSIDGE, and in the Parish of Birstall, consisting of a Messuage, with a Barn, Stable, Shops and other Conveniences, and Thirty Days Work of Land, late in the Possession of Mr. Broadley's Executors.

☞ Particulars may be known by applying to Mr. Gomersall, of Birstall.

To be LETT,

A MESSUAGE called SCAR-HILL, consisting of a Dining-Room and Two Parlours, a very good Kitchen, back Kitchen, (with a Pump and Plenty of very good Water in) and Brewhouse, Five good Lodging Rooms, and Three Garrets, Barn, Stables, Warehouses, and other convenient Outbuildings, and about Thirty-two Days Work of Land in a ring Fence adjoining to the Building.

*** SCAR-HILL is in a very pleasant and healthy Situation, commanding an extensive Prospect, and very suitable for a Gentleman, Merchant, capital Wooll-stapler, or Manufacturer, being within the Distance of One Mile and a Half from Bradford, Eight Miles from Leeds, Eight Miles from Halifax, Twelve Miles from Huddersfield, and Eight Miles from Otley, all good Market Towns, and adjoining to a good Turnpike Road.

The Land may be entered to at Candlemas, and the Buildings at May-Day next, or sooner if required.

☞ The present Tenant will shew the Premises, and further Particulars may be had by applying to Messrs. Atkinsons, Bradford.

To be SOLD by AUCTION,

Together or in Separate LOTS,

At the White-Lion, in Halifax, on Monday the 26th Day of February Instant, at Four in the Afternoon, situate in Southowram, near Halifax,

A MESSUAGE and FARM-HOUSE, with the Barns, Stables, Cow-Houses, and other convenient Outbuildings, and Five Closes of Land contiguous and near thereto, containing together about Twenty-one Days Work, in the Possession of Abraham Fox.

Also several HOUSES in the Possessions of Thomas Turner, Samuel Farrer, Thomas Moorhouse, John Tattersall, and James Hollas.

The Housing is in good Repair, and the Lands in excellent Condition.

☞ Further Particulars may be had of Mr. John Foster, at Peacock-House, near Halifax; Mr. Joshua Waddington, at Park-Nook, in Southowram; or at Mr. Parker's Office, in Halifax.

This Day is published, Price 2s.

Sold at the Printing-Office, New-Street-End, Leeds; and may be had of all the Distributors of this Paper,

A TREATISE on the Nature, Symptoms, and Cure of the VENEREAL DISEASE: To which are subjoined, Observations on *Tabes Dorsalis*, Gleets, seminal Weaknesses, Impotence, Barenness, and the other ill Effects of secret or excessive Venery.——The twenty-first Edition, much enlarged and improved.

By J. SMYTH, M. D.

To be had of the Author, Great Suffolk-street, Charing-Cross; and also of Axtel, No. 1, Finch-lane, Cornhill; Pridden, No. 100, Fleet-street; Cavil, Middle-row, Holborn; Tilly, London-Bridge; Steel, Union-Row, Tower-Hill; and the other Venders of the Doctor's Medicines in Great-Britain and Ireland.

The Restorative for all Persons labouring under any of the various deplorable Concomitants of a broken and decayed Constitution is in Bottles of 11s. od. and the Specific at 5s. 5d. and 2s. 9d. each.

STATE-LOTTERY for 1786.

Begins drawing the 12th of Feb. 1787.

MR. HODGES begs Leave to inform the Public, That he has an office at No. 124, under the late Royal Academy in Pall-Mall, London, (appointed by Government) where are now on sale a variety of Tickets and Shares, divided into Halves, Quarters, Eighths, and Sixteenths, and legally stamped pursuant to act of parliament.

Mr HODGES flatters himself that the probity that has hitherto directed all his negociations, and the punctuality with which he has answered every demand, amounting abstractedly in capital prizes to the immense sum of 325,000l. will confirm the confidence he has been uniformly assiduous to obtain. The capital prizes (a list of which is too numerous to be inserted in this advertisement) may be seen at his Majesty's Exchequer, with the name of *Hodges* endorsed thereon. One capital prize in particular, Mr Hodges thinks it essential to specify, which is No. 22,117, sold in four quarters to the following gentlemen, viz. Mr Adams, in Pall-Mall, London; Mr Machelli, in the Haymarket, London; Mr Gaunt, in Abingdon-street, Westminster; and Mr Read, at the Salt-Office, Glocester, in the Lottery 1781, and drawn a prize of *Twenty Thousand Pounds*.

Letters (post paid) from country correspondents duly answered; and none but good bills at sight or short date will be taken; and money sent in small parcels by the coach, with full directions, will come safe to hand.

A CAUTION to the PUBLIC.

There is now an act of parliament in full force which makes it illegal, and, consequently, prohibits the sale of all sorts of Chances or Policies whatsoever, and makes that mode of adventuring by persons who keep shops, either in London or any country town in the kingdom, under the fallacious or assumed title of Lottery-offices, (whether as principals or agents in that species of illicit traffic) and both the agents, as well as principals, liable to the penalty of 50l. for every chance or policy vended by either party. But for the better information of the public in general, there will be *another* act of parliament passed before the drawing of the present lottery commences in February next, which will make the sellers in London, and all country agents, liable to much heavier pains and penalties than they are subject to under the present act.

THE OLD
Leeds and Newcastle Diligence,

SETS out from the Star-and-Garter Inn, Leeds, every Evening about Seven o'Clock, and from Mr TURNER's, the Queen's Head, Pilgrim Street, Newcastle, every Evening at the same Hour; meets at the King's Head, Northallerton, every Morning, and arrives at Leeds and Newcastle, every Day to Dinner.

☞ At Newcastle, this Carriage meets the Edinbro' Light Coach, with Four Horses, which goes out every Evening.—At Leeds, meets the London, Sheffield, Nottingham, Birmingham, Bristol, Bath, Plymouth, Halifax, Manchester, and Liverpool Coaches, which go out every Day; and in which Places are reserved for all Passengers coming in this Conveyance.

The Proprietors have fixed this Carriage upon such a Plan, as to render the travelling in it *perfectly safe*; and full as expeditious as the *Mail Coach, although they pay both Duty and Turnpikes*.

Fare from LEEDS to NEWCASTLE 1l. 8s. od.

Performed by { WOOD, Leeds.
GOODLAD, Harrogate,
HADDON, Ripon.
BULMER, Northallerton.
HOULT, Durham.
TURNER, Newcastle.

The Proprietors will not be accountable for any Parcel, Box or Truss, above Five Pounds Value, unless entered and paid for accordingly.

To be SOLD,

(By PRIVATE CONTRACT)

TEN FREEHOLD MESSUAGES or DWELLING-HOUSES, pleasantly situate opposite the Vicarage in Kirkgate, in Leeds, and Three Stables, with suitable Conveniences thereto belonging, in the Possessions of Robert Wray and Others.

ALSO, Twenty-seven FREEHOLD DWELLING-HOUSES or TENEMENTS, situate at Hill-house Bank, in Leeds aforesaid, in the Possession of Cha. Radcliffe and others.

ALSO, A Small PIECE of GROUND, containing about One Rood, at Hill-house Bank aforesaid, wherein is a good Bed of Clay.

☞ All the above Premises are in exceeding good Repair, and well tenanted.

For further Particulars apply to Mr. Thomas Shepley, at Mr. Shepley's Office, in Leeds.

WAKEFIELD, February 2, 1787.

AT a respectable Meeting of Justices of the Peace, Clergy, Gentlemen, and others, held here this Day, for the Purpose of taking into Consideration Mr. Gilbert's intended Bill, respecting the Poor Laws,

It is unanimously Resolved,

That this Plan of Mr Gilbert is projected upon so large and complicated a Scale, as to defeat its own Purpose.

That the necessary Load of Business which is to be imposed upon so many Individuals, and who are *compellable*, under certain Penalties, to undertake it, cannot possibly be endured.

That it will prove highly oppressive upon the Poor who are the Objects of it.

That Justices of the Peace, in Matters relative to the Poor, will be hereby rendered the mere Ministers of Office, to levy Penalties and Forfeitures, or to preside at a Ballot.

That so far from *preventing* Disputes between Parishes, it may be *productive* of endless Litigation.

That the immediate and consequential Expences thereof, will amount to an enormous Sum, a Sum beyond any Idea of reasonable Computation.

That the whole System of the Poor Laws will be shaken to its very Foundation, because not less than Thirty Acts of Parliament must be revised, or repealed, and most of them founded on the *good old Law of Queen Elizabeth*, of which that eminent Judge *Sir William Blackstone*, speaks in the following strong and decided Terms:

"A Plan was formed in the Reign of Queen Elizabeth, "more humane and beneficial, than even feeding and "cloathing of Millions, by affording the Poor the "Means (with proper Industry) to feed and cloath "themselves. And the further any subsequent Plans "for maintaining the Poor have departed from this Institution, the more *impracticable*, and even *pernicious*, "their *visionary Attempts* have proved."

Resolved therefore, That the Resolutions come to by this Meeting, be sent to the two Members for this County; and that they be desired to use their best Endeavours to prevent the passing of Mr. Gilbert's Bill into a Law; and that such Resolutions be also transmitted to the Members for the City of York, and the Boroughs within the County, and to such other Members of the House of Commons, as the Chairman may think proper.

That the Chairman be empowered to call a General Meeting of the Gentlemen, Clergy, Freeholders, and Inhabitants of the West Riding of Yorkshire, whenever in his Opinion it shall be necessary to take Mr. Gilbert's Bill in[illegible]ther Consideration.

That the Thanks of the Meeting be give[illegible] ovidence D[illegible]an.

H. ZOUC[illegible]

THURSDAY's POST.

LONDON, *February* 6.

YESTERDAY in the House of Lords, the Marquis of Carmarthen moved for a copy of the convention with his Catholic Majesty, and several papers ascertaining the amount of the imports and exports from and to France, from the 14th of January 1784, to the 14th day of the same month 1787, to be laid before their Lordships; which motions were severally agreed to.

Yesterday in the House of Commons, the Chancellor of the Exchequer moved, without any preface, that the House resolve itself on Monday next into a committee, to take into consideration that part of his Majesty's speech which relates to the Treaty of Commerce with France.

Lord Mulgrave seconded the motion; but

Lord George Cavendish, sen. moved by way of amendment, that Monday fortnight be substituted in its stead.—This brought on a debate, in which

Mr Fox charged the Minister with precipitation in calling upon the House so suddenly to decide upon a business of such magnitude as the commercial treaty. Similar precipitation, he said, had marked the Minister's conduct in the business of the Irish propositions, which had like to have been hurried through parliament, before the manufacturers could obtain time to give in evidence the numerous and strong objections they had against them. The Minister, he observed, ought not to be in a hurry; he ought to know the sentiments of Ireland relative to the commercial treaty, as it was optional in the parliament of that kingdom to adopt or reject it. He stated that there was a rumor about town; which he could call only a rumor, though he himself had not a doubt of its being well-founded—that the Court of Lisbon had rejected the propositions made by Great Britain, so that there was an end to the negociations between this country and Portugal. He thought a short delay, at least, and a call of the House highly necessary on so momentous an occasion.

The Chancellor of the Exchequer replied, that the charge of precipitation was ill founded; neither Parliament nor the nation could be said to be taken by surprize, when called upon to consider on Monday next a Treaty which had been already four months before the public. Gentlemen must, by this time, be fully acquainted with the sentiments of their constituents on the Commercial Treaty, therefore they could have no occasion for any delay or a call of the House. Great apprehensions were entertained about our connexion with Portugal. He would not conceal from the Hon. Gentleman, that the French Treaty would inevitably occasion an essential change in our commerce with that country. He was indeed sollicitous to bring forward the question, that he might have an opportunity of demonstrating how well the Treaty is calculated in all its views and aspects, to do away the objections which have been urged against it. Whether it tended to annihilate the Methuen Treaty or not, he was certain it would stand on its own principles; and he was prepared to vindicate its contents under all these disadvantages. He allowed that it had occasioned more difficulty in our negociations with the Court of Portugal, than were expected; and that, on account of this proposed connection with France, that Court insisted on our reducing the duties on her wines one third. He would not now state how far it was proper or improper to comply with such terms. He was willing to take the matter just as the Hon. Gentleman seemed disposed to estimate it, and even allowing his hypothesis to extend to a final rupture with Portugal, he thought himself, notwithstanding all these concessions, perfectly qualified to rest the whole on the issue of fair argument.

In regard, however, to the report, he would say that no final answer had as yet arrived from Lisbon; but he believed that the Portuguese Minister at our court was authorised to negociate a Plan of Commerce advantageous to the two countries.

After another debate, in which Sir Richard Hill, Mr. Francis, Mr Wilbraham, and Mr. Burke, took a part, the House divided on Lord George Cavendish's amendment, when there appeared, Ayes 89; Noes, 211; Majority against the amendment, 124.

Mr. Pitt's motion was then put and carried without a division.

In the House of Commons this day, Mr Steele presented "a list of pensions, together with the names of the persons to whom the same are granted since the 6th of February 1786, pursuant to an act of the 22d of his present Majesty." The title was read, and the list ordered to lie on the table.

A motion was made, "That an account of the number of seamen and marines borne and mustered each month from the first day of January 1786, to the 31st day of December 1786, inclusive, be laid before this House."

Yesterday arrived a mail from Jamaica, brought to Falmouth by the Halifax packet, in five weeks.

Yesterday morning the Lord Chancellor and Mr. Pitt, had a private conference with his Majesty, at the Queen's Palace, when the following law arrangements were agreed upon. Mr. Serjeant Grose to be the Puisne Judge of the King's Bench, vacant by the death of the late Justice Willes. Alexander Thompson, Esq; Accountant-General, to be Puisne Baron of the Exchequer, vacant by James Eyre, Esq; promoted to the Chief Baronship. And Serjeant Walker to be Accountant-General, in the room of Mr. Thompson made a Judge.

The Lord Lieutenant of Ireland has signifyed to Government here, that the troops intended as re-enforcements for those now in that kingdom, will not be wanted.

Yesterday the new appointed Bishops of New-[illegible]k and Philadelphia were consecrated at Lambeth [illegible], and this day are to set off for America.

Letters received from Berlin, by Saturday's Dut[illegible]h mail, give to understand that his Prussian Majesty is by no means pleased at the resistance opposed by the Stadtholder to the overtures made to him for a reconciliation with the States of Holland. Baron G[illegible] who had in vain exerted all his persuasive powe[illegible] bring it about, is positively recalled, and it seem[illegible] if the King of Prussia was determined not to inte[illegible] any more in the disputes between his brother-i[illegible] and the aforesaid States.

If advices from the Continent may be cre[illegible] there seems to be something of an approaching [illegible]lution among the French Ministry. The Count[illegible] Vergennes is said to be at the point of death. The Duke de la Vauguyon has been sent for in a great hurry to court, as is supposed to succeed him; and the Marchioness of Polignac is dismissed from her attendance [illegible]bout the Princesses.

An Eighteenth Century Newspaper. (*Courtesy of The British Newspaper Archive*) and distributing information, or when a publication was on a small scale, a newspaper's editor rarely owned the paper. The creative aspects of writing copy and the hard-headed negotiations essential for running a business were not necessarily found in one person. Many successful newspapers were either set up or rescued by an entrepreneur who had spotted a gap in the market and tailored a product to fit it. By the start of the twentieth century, a proprietor could own a web of apparently unconnected titles.

The function of a proprietor was to provide the business plan and secure the finance to make the paper a commercial success. This included salaries for staff involved in news-gathering and editing and the typesetting and printing costs, whether as an in-house activity or at an independent printers.

The owner of a newspaper had legitimate business reasons for wanting to guide its tone and content. When there was more than one title in a portfolio a proprietor did not want them competing for the same readers or advertisers. Sometimes though, newspaper magnates had personal ambitions to influence the conduct of public affairs and used their newspapers to promote their own agenda. Scrutinising how a government carried out its duties had been accepted as a legitimate function of a free press since the later decades of the nineteenth century. At the start of the twentieth century, the press barons of the age trod very dangerous ground in some of the criticisms they levelled through the pages of their newspapers at the elected politicians who were grappling with difficult problems. They were eventually denounced for trying to exercise power without responsibility and gradually stepped back into a more orthodox business role of defining the tone for a newspaper and expecting the editor to deliver it, rather than actively dictating what was included.

Editors

The most significant role at a newspaper was that of its editor-in-chief who was held responsible for everything it printed. Usually, the person appointed to this challenging job had worked as a journalist and understood how news was collected and published. Editorship always involved some personal risk and, in the eighteenth and nineteenth centuries, an editor could easily find himself in court and possibly in prison for various crimes against the state if his paper printed something that annoyed the establishment. Even when criminality was not involved, individuals who thought their reputations had been harmed by a report regularly resorted to libel actions against newspapers, sometimes leading to an award of damages.

An editor carried out several functions. One was to position the newspaper in the market place, which could be a delicate balancing act between pleasing the proprietor, pleasing advertisers and pleasing customers. Specific tasks included commissioning reporters and other contributors, writing or authorising editorial articles and deciding what was to be published. The editor-in-chief of a large paper probably delegated routine decisions about what news to include, or how to edit an article, to experienced deputies but would have been closely involved with anything that might prove contentious. He may have personally written some of the paper's editorial articles (known as 'leaders') and would have closely scrutinised any material that was written in his name.

Journalists and Writers

Eighteenth century newspapers received plenty of news by letter, from a network of correspondents based in Britain or scattered around the globe. Some of these correspondents forwarded letters they had received from friends, relatives and business acquaintances and it is not clear how much early copy was ever intended to find its way into the public domain. When a newspaper became established it might have invested in salaried journalists to collect some types of news, such as the proceedings in Parliament, whilst relying on freelance suppliers for stories from more distant parts.

Until the middle of the nineteenth century, detailed accounts of some court proceedings may have been provided by solicitors who had sent junior clerks to record decisions being taken in courts around the country, so that their legal practice could be as informed as possible about any new developments. Selling a copy of their notes to newspapers helped to defray the travel and accommodation costs the clerks had incurred.

It was not unusual for news to be worded identically in newspapers that were not in the same group. There was no pretence of exclusivity and some freelance journalists managed to sell the same copy to several editors well into the nineteenth century. Nor were newspapers reticent about plagiarism, as they routinely copied interesting stories from other publications verbatim, perhaps with an acknowledgement of the source. By the 1850s, some journalists marketed their stories to a press agency which collected news from around the world and supplied it to any papers who paid for it on a non-exclusive basis.

A Nineteenth Century Newspaper. (*Courtesy of* The Barnsley Chronicle)

Until the twentieth century, journalists were anonymous as newspapers did not include a by-line to show who had written the piece. This makes it impossible to be sure exactly how the news supply chain operated at any point but the differing treatments of the same news, and the variety of detail that is mentioned in reports from around 1860 onwards, suggests that copy was becoming more exclusive to a single paper or group in the latter part of the nineteenth century. Faster transport had made it feasible to despatch a salaried member of staff to cover a developing story, rather than hoping that someone who was already there would send in a report. The telegraph and the telephone allowed an editor to agree a commission with a reporter who was based in the locality of a story to cover it on an exclusive basis.

Alongside reporters who covered the news as it broke, or carried out investigations, were writers who researched and wrote features and articles on specific topics. Some of these were penned by freelance journalists who developed specialisms and sold exclusive pieces to whoever commissioned them, but subject experts with a good writing style were also able to find a market for articles that fell within their personal field of expertise. Authors of fiction were also regular freelance contributors and, even in the nineteenth century, this market was open to women.

Illustrators and Photographers

From the middle of the nineteenth century, artists gradually joined journalists as an essential part of the news chain with the development of illustrated newspapers. The role of an artist in the field was essentially the same as that of a reporter and many seem to have worked on a freelance basis, furnishing sketches from the scene that could be translated into print. Staff artists who were expert woodcarvers or metal etchers were retained by newspapers to carry out the specialised tasks of carving an outline drawing onto a block of wood, which was in turn used to create a metal plate for use in printing.

As the nineteenth century progressed, photography joined sketching as a way of providing the initial images for a woodcarver and etcher to work from. During the twentieth century, when it became possible to use photographic negatives in the printing process, the camera gradually took over as the method of capturing the images which illustrated the news. Work for the newspaper artist declined but new opportunities opened out for photographers to cover everything from a local fund raising garden party through to major national and international events.

A Twentieth Century Newspaper. (*Courtesy of* The Barnsley Chronicle)

Desk Editors

Several experienced journalists, perhaps known as sub-editors or copy editors, or anyone who specialised in particular aspects of a newspaper's content, were based in the newspaper offices rather than out in the field. Their time was spent processing the steady flow of information from staff and freelance contributors. Tasks included checking the copy to make sure that it was easy to understand, perhaps rewording it to make it clearer for a reader, shortening reports that were too long for the space available, or combining them when there were several similar items to include. When newspaper headlines came into use towards the end of the nineteenth century, in response to the lower levels of literacy amongst some readers, desk editors would have been involved in creating the pithy captions that introduced a story. The more senior staff would have taken routine decisions about which reports to include and may have been involved in drafting editorial on behalf of the editor. Those with a subject specialism may have written articles and features.

The most responsible task for the journalistic staff who worked in any newspaper office was to ensure that the story was accurate and that the newspaper would not be breaking any laws or risking a libel claim by publishing it. Anything that was in any way contentious would have been referred on to the editor-in-chief for a decision about how to proceed, whether this was to pull the story, consult a lawyer, or publish and be damned.

Compositors and Printers

Newspapers were printed from large blocks, each the size of a page. Usually the page was split into perhaps six or eight columns, which were easier to read than a text that went right across the paper and allowed space to be used more productively. It also allowed printing blocks to be partly created in advance with a skeleton layout, where advertising or puzzles could be inserted as soon as they became available. Many papers reserved part of a column for news that broke close to the printing deadline.

Typesetting was a skilled job for manual workers who were excellent readers and deft with their hands and compositing was a well-paid occupation. Compositors performed the time-consuming, fiddly and physically arduous task of crafting the printing blocks from loose, pre-formed images of letters, or perhaps words for ones that were used regularly. The first task was to produce

Compositor's Letters
used to form Newspaper
Text. (*Author's collection*)

individual articles in block form, from the written reports that were sent through to them. These small blocks were then combined to create the master printing block. By the mid-nineteenth century, some papers had risen to the challenge of producing illustrations that could be included in a printing block, alongside typeset written material.

Compositing could be a pressurised job when a print deadline was approaching, especially if important copy had only just arrived. Accuracy was essential and speed could not be increased by having more hands working on a block. By the end of the nineteenth century, mechanisation was replacing the traditional manual method of typesetting and making the process much faster. It was an essential advance for a newspaper that wanted to publish daily and to be as up-to-date as possible.

In the nineteenth century, compositors helped their newspapers to develop a distinctive visual identity with typefaces that were easy to read and layouts that were consistent across editions. When Stamp Duty had been high, the priority was to cram as much onto a page as possible, irrespective of aesthetics or ease of reading. With taxes reduced and newspapers being produced daily, page layout became less crushed and more dependent on a compositor's skill and artistic eye to produce something visually pleasing but which did not waste valuable space.

When all the page blocks had been compiled, responsibility passed from the compositor to the printer. Printing equipment developed rapidly in the nineteenth century but the essential process was that the block was coated with ink, which stuck to the raised surface of each letter. Sheets of paper were then pressed onto the inked plates, whether manually or mechanically, and the writing appeared on the paper.

The role of compositors and printers can be overlooked but without their skills, which were entirely different to those of the people who gathered and wrote the news, it would have been impossible to take the news to market. The marriage of several diverse talents was necessary to produce a good newspaper.

Distribution

Even when a pile of newspapers stood hot off the press not everyone in the news chain could relax. There was still one more task to complete. Getting the paper into the hands of the customer was a big logistical undertaking, which was essential for the viability of the business. Although some revenue would have been received from the many people who inserted advertisements in the paper, the new copies had to be made available for paying customers before they contained yesterday's news.

The first newspapers had relatively small print runs. Their main outlet was in the burgeoning coffee houses of the capital and provincial towns where they were available for the patrons to peruse. Unless the printing press was local, the method of distribution was by stage coach. These did not necessarily run to all places every day, so it was a matter of luck whether an edition arrived on time, some days late, or not at all. Unreliable distribution networks are one reason why newspapers had tended to print just one or two editions a week. They also explain why provincial newspapers were so successful. Printing close to the market was the most practical method of disseminating the news.

From the 1840s, the railways transformed newspaper distribution. Large and heavy bundles of papers could be moved quickly and reliably on trains that ran to the same daily time-table, stimulating businessmen to set up as wholesalers in large towns and to create local distribution networks that delivered a batch of copies to newsagents. Stations themselves became part of the retail supply chain. William Henry Smith, whose family already operated a newsagent's business, opened a bookstall at Euston Station in 1848. His innovation quickly spread to many other stations in the next decade.

Not all customers could be relied upon to collect their newspaper every day and, anticipating irregular purchases, retailers developed a home delivery service, ensuring that the customer received, and paid for, a newspaper every day. Street vendors were also a part of the process, picking up the casual custom of passers-by.

Distribution arrangements had to be slick and robust, getting the paper from the publisher to the customer in a matter of hours. Newspapers had a very short shelf life, perhaps just a day, before the next edition superseded them. There were a multiplicity of titles on offer from the 1850s, making competition fierce. If the preferred newspaper did not arrive on time, there were plenty of others to tempt the reader.

Conclusion

Newspapers were an integral part of the society that produced them and reflected its values, concerns and diversity. The process of transferring the news from where it happened to the paying customer was a complicated process that involved several stages and many skills. Appreciating how the industry functioned at the time a newspaper was printed, helps to enrich it as a source.

Chapter 3

Content of a Newspaper

Newspapers have always featured much more than events which had taken place since the previous edition went to press. They gave their customers a broad package of reading matter that included news, comment, announcements, public notices, articles, reviews, letters from readers, gossip, illustrations, cartoons and advertisements. They also provided entertainment through stories, serials, poetry, puzzles and competitions. By including a variety of content, editors aimed to attract a large number of readers and the advertising income which they needed to thrive.

Editorial

The word editorial refers to the opinions expressed by the most senior staff of a newspaper. It relates to some news that is reported in that edition of the paper but it tends to be printed separately from the topic it is commenting on. Editorial usually reflects the values that the paper and, by extension, its readership hold. It often seeks to influence the reader's opinion by drawing out lessons, asking questions, or advocating change. At times of crisis, editorials may try to unite the readership by arguing that no other course of action is possible. On happy occasions, such as a national celebration or major scientific advance, an editorial may explain why the event is so special and try to predict how it will be regarded in the future.

Newspapers began to develop a distinctive editorial voice during the nineteenth century as official attitudes towards the press became more relaxed. As the century progressed, some newspaper editors pioneered a new, unofficial, role for a free press: holding the government and official institutions to account for their stewardship of the country and perhaps calling for change.

Editorial articles provide insight into what educated people (usually male), thought were the important issues of their day. How far editorial reflects the wider public mood is debatable and it is not always clear whether an editor is simply reflecting the readers' views, or actually trying to steer them in a particular direction. Many people were more concerned with the practicalities of everyday life than with an issue that did not affect them directly and may have felt indifferent towards some topics that enthused journalists and politicians. Whatever stance an editorial took, it is always worth checking other papers to discover the both sides of an argument. Irish newspapers, for example, interpret the troubles at the beginning of the twentieth century very differently to British newspapers.

As editorial is opinion, it may present an unbalanced view; points can be emphasised or excluded to create the desired impression. Sometimes an opinion may have been presented as though it were fact, drawing the reader into a certain way of thinking.

Example

It is a truth universally acknowledged, that a single man in possession of a good fortune, must be in want of a wife.

Jane Austen, Pride and Prejudice, 1813

Austen's famous opening line is an example of opinion being portrayed as fact. There is no evidence to support either the truth of the assertion that a single man in possession of a good fortune must be in want of a wife, or that everyone acknowledges this is the case.

Most editorial in newspapers well-regarded for their quality is authoritative and well-argued, but there are instances of muddled thinking and convoluted writing even in these papers. Before relying on any piece of editorial for evidence, ensure that it is good quality journalism. If it is hard to express the meaning in modern language it may have meant little when it was written.

> **Example**
>
> On the eve of Queen Victoria's Diamond Jubilee *The Times* described the bonds between Britain and her overseas colonies as:
>
> *so subtle as to baffle the analysis of utilitarians and cynics. They almost elude the observation even of the imaginative and the sympathetic. Yet their reality is proved by the tests they have undergone, by the centrifugal tendencies they have proved strong enough to resist and by the growing moral and material consolidation that is being carried out under their influence.*
>
> The Times 19th June 1897
>
> The concept that became known as Imperialism was firmly established in Britain by 1897 but this vague wording merits a question about how well *The Times* understood it.

Editors usually commented on significant news rather than mundane items, so their choices may point to unexpected lines of research. If an editor found the outcome of an apparently routine court case important enough to highlight, or drew attention to a standard charitable activity, there may be something in the news story that merits closer investigation.

News

Up-to-date information about recent happenings formed the largest element in most newspapers, usually concentrating on certain types of event. The actions of Parliament and government and proceedings in court cases were routinely included. Reports of war or conflict, serious accidents and crime also featured prominently. Alongside these staple items, there was plenty of detailed economic news reflecting the on-going importance of commercial and business knowledge to a significant proportion of readers. Ample space was allocated to information about the weather, especially at sowing and harvest times, which shows how many people were once involved in some form of agriculture.

Sport has always received regular coverage. Initially this concentrated on activities such as horse racing that were regarded as a gentleman's recreation.

Over time, these were joined by reports of professional matches played by the new sports teams that were followed by many working men. Cultural pastimes were frequently noted, in theatre and concert reviews, as well as critiques of new publications and the latest paintings to be hung in exhibition halls. In the twentieth century, material broadcast by the new and popular mediums of radio and television was routinely previewed and reviewed.

Newspapers reported negative stories more often than positive ones. The majority of the news focussed on situations where something had gone wrong, or on people who had flouted the prevailing codes of conduct. This can create a false impression of what life was really like and the values of ordinary people. Good news was included in many papers but tucked away on an inside page or only mentioned briefly. One benefit now accruing from digitised newspapers is the ability to search for the positive stories, to help to redress the balance.

There are always days when the news is more varied than others. A major disaster, key political developments, a high profile crime, national celebrations, or the death of an important public figure all generate copious coverage, reducing the space available for other news. An internal memo sent in the Department of Transport on 11 September 2001 by a government advisor whilst the destruction of the World Trade Centre in New York was unfolding, to the effect that the day would be a good one to bury bad news, perfectly illustrates this.

When major stories break, they may limit the range of news coverage for several days, as attention focuses on the central and the peripheral aspects of the story. Conversely, on the days with a dearth of important news to report, trivial or frivolous items may be included, just to fill space. Slow-news days are interesting to research as they can offer better insight into the everyday lives and concerns of ordinary people than ones when there were major stories to print.

Investigations

Investigations were specific to the newspaper that commissioned them and involved detailed research using multiple sources. They were usually carried out by an experienced journalist who worked on a subject for a period of time before writing a report. On occasions, the investigation resulted in a series of related articles that pulled no punches and then called for official action to address identified problems. Influential investigations by newspapers included the reports in *The Times* in 1855 about the mismanagement of the military campaign in the Crimea and *The Pall Mall Journal*'s exposure of child prostitution in 1885.

Investigation reports are valuable historical evidence, as they were usually researched by very competent investigators who sourced and collated a substantial amount of information to establish the current position. As such, they are very helpful for understanding social or economic conditions. They can also assist with topics that have never been studied in detail by historians, or included in reference books.

Investigations into emotive subjects have generated powerful and persuasive pieces of writing but this does not mean that any, however influential it may have been, stands above challenge. An investigator who became a passionate advocate for a course of action may have succumbed to the temptation to distort any findings. This could include practices such as presenting single or extreme instances as the norm, making unwarranted generalisations, or omitting any mention of mitigating factors.

Campaigns

By the mid-nineteenth century, newspapers began to take on the role of public conscience, and became involved in local and national campaigns for change. One tactic was to include articles or editorials highlighting a particular problem. An early example was the demand for government action in 1842, when a shocking official report exposed the degrading treatment of some women and children who worked in coal mines. Local newspapers also used their influence to support issues that had become important to their readers, possibly because the readers expected it. An interesting facet of this campaigning role is the way newspapers sometimes became involved with calls for more humane treatment of prisoners facing sentences that members of the public thought were excessive.

Features

Features and specialist articles flourished as the tax on newspapers was reduced. They range from serious pieces that discuss a newsworthy topic in detail, to an ongoing series about a popular subject where there was always knowledge to be shared. Scientific discoveries, technological progress, changing fashions, gardening, cookery, travel and motoring were often covered in a regular weekly

Fashions in 1890. (*Author's Collection*)

feature, which is now very useful for dating change and development. As literacy increased and more than one person read the family newspaper, some publications responded with the introduction of a women's page or a children's corner. Many also introduced intellectual challenge with crosswords and word puzzles, chess and bridge problems.

Fiction

Fiction was also a regular component of newspapers from the eighteenth century. It gradually found a home in magazines, though some newspapers printed stories into the twentieth century; an indication that some readers wanted more from a newspaper than just the news. Fiction was often published in episodic form and an exciting serial could turn into a good marketing tool. The hallmark of an effective serial was that each episode ended at a point of tension or high drama, tempting the reader to buy the next edition to discover what happened next. It was an effective business strategy. News was common to other papers but fiction was a unique selling point.

Births, Marriages and Deaths

Although family notices and related news items do not occupy much space in a newspaper they provide plenty of valuable information for several types of research. Most local newspapers and some national ones included listings of births, marriages and deaths and other personal details, such as engagements, wedding anniversaries and remembrance of the deceased. Occasionally, an old newspaper lists baptisms, weddings or funerals sourced from church registers. In the twentieth century, the professional photographer who had taken the nuptial pictures sometimes sent a shot of the bride and groom to the local paper, as a way of publicising his business.

Family announcements are not always straightforward as they often specify the day on which an event occurred rather than the date, making it necessary to check when the paper was published and then count backwards to discover when it happened. For bereavement, the paper may have noted the date of the funeral rather than the death. The words *inst*, meaning this, and *ult*, meaning previous, were sometimes used in family announcements.

Newspapers can provide family historians with information that does not come to light through other records, such as the birth and death of a child in the period between the ten-yearly censuses. They may also reveal a prior marriage for an ancestor and time spent as a widow or widower. Sometimes the insights are more subtle. As family announcements were paid for by the person who inserted them, tributes at death and memorial notices on an anniversary of a death from someone other than a member of the person's immediate family can provide clues about relationships, feelings and personalities.

The marriages of middle-class couples were regularly reported as a news item and these can yield valuable details about the family, such as the names of the bridesmaids, best man and gentleman ushers, and their relationship to the bridal pair. Occasionally the wedding guests were listed. The bride's dress and flowers and those of her retinue may have been described, along with details of the reception and where the newly-weds were spending their honeymoon. Descendants of the couple are not the only researchers who may be interested in this information. Anyone studying costume, or the social context of marriage, can find detail that helps to create a picture of the times, or of changing times.

When significant individuals died, newspapers routinely included obituaries which summarised their life. Obituaries can reveal life stories that have been forgotten by descendants over time. Tributes at death often included comments about the deceased's achievements or how they were regarded by contemporaries. These should be treated with caution, especially if they vary from other sources. Negative aspects of character are rarely mentioned immediately after someone has died.

Letters from Readers

Reader's letters have been staple content of newspapers from inception to the present day. Indignant, irascible, questioning or quirky letters offer a valuable glimpse of what was important to individual readers. Relying on a letter in isolation to demonstrate anything other than the writer's own point of view, should be undertaken with caution. It is likely that a single letter could be found in a newspaper, somewhere, to support any contention, however absurd.

Always check more than one publication before drawing conclusions about public opinion from reader's letters. Even when several letters making the same point were published in a newspaper, it is impossible to know how far this did represent a wider public feeling, because twice as many expressing the opposite viewpoint could have been ignored by the editor. In the twentieth century, newspapers generally tried to present a balanced selection of readers' views, but in the nineteenth century, editors were less keen on material that expressed dissent or challenged the official standpoint.

Some correspondents were happy for their own name to be attached to a letter but others withheld it or adopted a pseudonym such as *Humanitas*, *The Children's Friend*, *Verax* or *Disgusted*. One reason for adopting an alias to conceal identity was because the writer was a well-known figure, actively involved in promoting, or resisting, a campaign for reform. The power of the press for influencing public opinion had been recognised and acted on at a very early stage. Another reason was that the views expressed were controversial and perhaps invited retribution.

Individuals who were in the public eye were more likely to have had a letter published in a newspaper than someone whose name, or public role, was not known. This included people who wrote to set the record straight when they felt they had been misrepresented by the newspaper in some way. It is always worth checking reader's correspondence if faced with a negative story about a person, as it is possible that they could have asked the editor to print a correction.

Only a very small number of people ever wrote to a newspaper. Those who did were predominantly well-heeled, educated, literate men and women who had the time to put pen to paper, often with a burning passion for their subject and the confidence to express their opinion in public. Working class readers were much less likely to have made their views known in this manner because, apart from the fact that many had a lower level of literacy, a culture of deference to the establishment persisted well into the twentieth century. This made many disinclined to put forward their own opinion if it challenged an accepted position and many others did not consider writing to a newspaper as something they were entitled to do.

Discovering a letter penned by an ancestor can be a significant find for a family historian and demonstrates that they felt very strongly about the issue. It does not necessarily reveal anything about their standard of literacy or writing style as the correspondence may have been edited into a grammatical format by the newspaper.

Advertising

Newspapers began as information sheets which publicised goods for sale and provided other content to attract a wider readership. Paid advertising soon developed into a major component of successful newspapers. Although it was easy to overlook the importance of advertising when devouring the news, without it, and the money it provided to the newspaper, most would not have been able to afford to publish all of their other content.

Advertising differs markedly from everything else in a newspaper in that it was paid for by whoever inserted the copy in order to influence readers to spend their money in a particular way. It was also independent of the editorial staff, which enhances its power as evidence of prevailing cultural values and of what mattered to different segments of the population.

Newspaper advertising was especially important until the late-twentieth century, as there were few other cost effective ways for a business to reach a large audience. With most readers having some money to spend at their discretion, it was a valuable tool for promoting products that needed a large number of customers to buy a small amount, rather than ones that were sold in quantity to a few other purchasers. Almost everything that could be sold legally at the relevant time may have been advertised in newspapers, from exotic foreign travel to local houses for sale or to rent. The latest in luxury clothing for well-heeled men and women featured, as well as mundane protective caps for the pit ponies that hauled coal along the underground passageways of the local mine.

Branded, unadulterated foodstuffs jostled for attention, alongside branded (as yet unproven) remedies for unspecified ailments suffered by men, women and children. Some advertisements for 'too good to be true' offers on gentlemen's pocket watches may have been the scams of their day, whilst reputable local jewellers pointed out that engagement rings were their business. The next instalment of Hollywood escapism at the local *Roxy* or *Odeon* proclaimed its credentials as an unmissable evening's entertainment, which could be followed by one of the many drinks that proclaimed itself a sleep-inducing nightcap.

Advertising was not homogeneous and took several forms. Classified advertising was relatively cheap and affordable to individuals as well as businesses. It was paid for by the line and at its peak, occupied multiple pages of the paper, perhaps a dozen or more. It comprised columns of short, almost identical, insertions, usually grouped by subject, such as *situations vacant*, *situations required* and *property to let*. Time-served tradesmen advertised their various crafts whilst *lost and found* enabled the careless to appeal for the return of missing property and the public spirited to try to reunite lost items and animals with their owner. Classified advertising can offer valuable pointers to economic conditions at national, regional or local level.

Initially advertising was found on the first pages of a paper, demonstrating its key role in providing revenue and perhaps making any controversial content less apparent. News stories were tucked away inside in whatever space was left. Some papers retained the practice of having advertising on the front page until until well into the twentieth century.

Advertisement for Hoods for Pit Ponies in the *Barnsley Chronicle*, 22 February 1912. (*Courtesy of the* Barnsley Chronicle)

Scattered throughout a newspaper, larger than classified advertisements and often incorporating a drawing and a few persuasive words, were notices about a wealth of consumer products that were placed by a manufacturer or retailer. This type of advertising is an excellent method of tracing the development of a product or service. Many of these advertisements mentioned a price which gives some indication of the presumed spending power of the likely purchaser.

Claims made about goods were not regulated, and advertisers were free to make unproven statements. Many products claimed health benefits that modern research can disprove, though the fact that an advertisement made a false claim was not necessarily dishonest at the time as the supplier may not have known better. Repeat business was important to manufacturers and retailers and a bad reputation was something most were keen to avoid, so deliberately misleading customers by lying about a product was not in a reputable supplier's interest.

Advertisers learned to pitch their product to a target buyer and to play on their emotions and values. Advertising of products that would interest a man concentrated on characteristics that marked him out as the soul of discernment, whatever his income. Food, cleaning and health-giving preparations and items for the home were targeted at women and the desire of a good wife and mother to give her family the best.

Some types of advertising were an informal information service so it made sense for newspapers to group similar items together. Anyone planning a visit to the cinema or theatre did not want to search through the paper hoping to spot every film or play and it was to the advantage of employers and potential employees, for job advertisements to be listed in a clearly identifiable section.

Advertising is an exceptional source for many types of research. By analysing advertisements, it is possible to build up a picture of life in a specific place at a specific time. Situations *vacant* which mention a salary and property to let with an indication of rent, gives insight into the earning power of local workers. Situations *wanted* on the other hand may yield information about the skills base in a locality and its labour supply. Theatre, cinema and entertainment listings show what was happening in provincial towns and villages, as opposed to what was happening in the large cities.

The lives of some people can be fleshed out through advertising. Theatrical entertainment was a peripatetic profession, but the movements and career of someone in a theatre company may be very precisely tracked through newspaper announcements of touring productions.

Conclusion

The different types of content in a newspaper will appeal to different types of researcher. Political historians can ascertain exactly how an important speech or government announcement was received, economic historians can build up a very detailed picture of an industry or a place and family historians can feel empathy with ancestors by reading the news as they would have read it, trying out a crossword or rediscovering a forgotten serial.

Digitised newspapers are a relatively new resource and one that is still becoming available. How this remarkably varied content can be used to reveal more about the past is an evolving process, and it seems probable that individual historians will devise some very innovative studies and unexpected methodologies in the coming years.

Chapter 4

Factors affecting Newspaper Research

A ll historical sources have benefits and drawbacks and newspapers are no exception. Being able to appreciate their strengths and limitations is essential for any researcher who wants to obtain the maximum benefit from this source and use it productively with other material.

Benefits of Newspapers

Accessibility

Until the twenty-first century, old newspapers were only available in archives and often only on microfilm. Reading equipment could be difficult to use and there were no search facilities to help locate relevant information, making it easy to miss something. Public archives are accessible to anyone but visiting them during their opening hours and being able to spend enough time to acquire the skills necessary for productive research with newspapers, could deter amateur historians from using them.

In less than a decade, this situation has completely changed. A large number of newspapers can now be searched on-line, at a time and place to suit an individual and this number is growing by the week. Not all on-line newspapers can be viewed for free but a subscription with a reputable provider should not price anyone out of the market and can be more cost-effective than travelling to an archive.

Best Source

Newspapers may be the best source of evidence available. This is certainly true when studying anything related to the history of newspapers, as they are the primary sources. Some issues that were of critical importance in the past have not been part of the modern world for many years and it is now difficult to find much information about them elsewhere. Newspapers can be excellent for revealing how ordinary people were affected by important events as this may have been overlooked by other sources.

Clarity

Newspapers were produced for a general readership, which did not necessarily have much time for reading. This meant that they were written in direct, plain language, which remains very comprehensible even after a century or more. They can provide a good way of starting to build up knowledge about a complex subject, for example, by highlighting the key recommendations of an official enquiry, or summarising a parliamentary debate.

Although newspapers offer excellent insight, they are never a substitute for any original source which is available, such as the enquiry report or the Hansard record of the parliamentary debate. Newspaper reports necessarily summarised and rarely present the full picture.

Completeness

In the past, manual searching made it impossible for any researcher to be sure that nothing relevant had been missed. As soon as a newspaper is digitised and can be searched electronically it is much less likely that a thorough and meticulous researcher will overlook something important.

Contemporaneous

The immediacy of publication means that when more than one paper independently included the same facts, their accuracy can usually be relied on. The story was still fresh in the reporter's mind, there was no opportunity for it to be influenced by hindsight and there was no time for pressure to be exerted to add or omit something. Accounts of the past, whether in history textbooks, memoirs or as anecdotes within families, tend to develop an 'accepted' version. They can also drift from what really happened with each retelling. This may be no more sinister than fading memory, or the narrator trying to express something succinctly but it can be intentional. Contemporaneous accounts fix the position.

Detail

Newspapers have captured and preserved a wealth of detail that was only of interest to their readers and would not have been recorded elsewhere. Some of this is human interest information that helps to show a person's character or feelings, or how a community reacted in the face of tragedy.

Diversity

Britain has long been a very diverse society, though this has not been well-reflected in some historical sources. Although their viewpoint tends to be middle-class, newspapers are excellent tool for identifying where diversity existed, and understanding the subtleties of how society functioned, from the eighteenth century onwards.

Empathy

Newspapers offer a way of seeing through another person's eyes. It is possible to discover what an ancestor or other person may have been reading at a key point in their lives, the influences they were exposed to, the technical developments that may have affected them and how they learned of such major events, as the relief of the siege of Mafeking in 1900 or the sinking of the Titanic in 1912.

New Discoveries

New sources always offer the prospect of making new discoveries. The amount of untapped material in old newspapers gives all historians an opportunity to carry out original studies or test currently held beliefs about the past. Some researchers find that working with new sources is much more satisfying than working with established ones.

Primary Sources

Newspapers are unrivalled for being able to investigate what was happening or what was considered important on a particular day. History text books inevitably pare subjects down to what authors and publishers think are the significant aspects. Newspapers can confirm or disprove that. They allow anyone interested in a topic to flesh out the detail and context.

Sole Source

Although other records would have been made at the time, some material has only survived in newspapers. Over the decades, a plethora of public and private organisations have been set up and then closed, merged, or transferred to new premises. In these situations, formal records of business have sometimes been lost, destroyed or now lie un-indexed in storage. A newspaper report of the discussions at one of the local boards set up in the nineteenth century may now be the only information about it.

Example

Bertram Wright and Frederick Sharp, youths residing at Crescent Road, Sheffield were summoned for furiously riding ponies at Cleethorpes on the 26th ult. They were fined 2s and 8s costs each.

Stamford Mercury 17th September 1897

This information about an ancestor and his best friend had not survived as oral history and may not be recorded anywhere else.

Sometimes there may never have been any other record. Reports of social functions, or the proceedings at a local society or a Sunday school prize-giving, are found in many local newspapers and may be of especial interest to family historians as they can provide information about an ancestor's life, interests and character.

Time Saving

Digital searching simplifies and speeds up the task of locating relevant material and reduces the probability of missing something significant. This enables a researcher to focus on analysis and drawing conclusions, rather than trawling microfilm or paper records to collect information.

Time Specific

Newspapers bear the date of their publication, which makes them an excellent way of establishing what was happening, or what was known, at a given time. This is valuable for cultural history as it enables the emergence and spread of ideas over time and in different parts of the country to be tracked with precision. Accurate dates can be very useful for establishing the chronology of how an aspect of law developed, tracking the career of a detective, local councillor or actor, or assessing the influence of a writer.

Pinpointing how any issue was understood at a given moment can give context to the manner in which governments and official agencies responded to unfolding problems or challenges. Actions that can seem inept with hindsight and a different value base, may not have been unreasonable at the time, given the information available to those who had to make the decision.

Practical Pitfalls

The value of newspapers as a historical source is enhanced when their limitations are understood. Pitfalls are not an insurmountable problem and when they are properly managed, quality research should result.

Completeness

Newspapers were produced to meet the needs of a contemporary readership, not to be a chronicle for future generations. Some news was never reported and sometimes the coverage was very brief. Whatever their publication date, newspapers can have frustrating, and sometimes fundamental, gaps for a modern researcher.

In the eighteenth century individuals were sometimes referred to as a lady, a gentleman, or by an occupation, or simply by the first letter of their surname. Forenames were often omitted. In the twentieth century, despite more personal details being included, it may still be impossible to confirm someone's identity.

Example

A great Lady has for some time been so very anxious to have a certain popular prisoner pardoned, that a message has been sent to him this week, that his pardon should shortly be granted; on which he observed, that unless it was free and unconditional, that he would not accept it.

Kentish Gazette 29th July 1769

At Derby Borough Court yesterday, James Boyle, described as a labourer, of Chellaston was ordered to pay 8s 6d inclusive or go to prison for seven days for being drunk and disorderly in the town early that morning.

Sheffield Evening Telegraph 26th October 1907

Despite the detail in the second report it is not sufficient to identify this man beyond reasonable doubt.

It may or may not be possible to discover more when a newspaper omits key details. As valuable research time can be consumed by an ultimately barren search, it is essential to acknowledge that on some occasions, persistence will not yield results.

Context

Historians using newspapers as a source are not reading them in the same manner as their original audience. The modern researcher has the benefit of knowing, or being able to discover, what happened next. Using evidence from a newspaper without properly understanding its context can each lead to false conclusions, whether about an ancestor or an aspect of society.

> **Example**
>
> In the 1890s, newspapers regularly reported the prosecution and jailing of working-class mothers, for neglecting their children. Individual reports reveal parents who squandered the weekly wages on alcohol whilst their children were dirty, underweight and ill-clad.
>
> A family historian might regretfully accept a neglectful Great-Grandmother at face value but, in some of these cases, the truth was different. The evidence that either or both parents squandered money on drink, was often an unsupported assertion made by middle-class officials, who had little idea of the cost of living for workers and thought anyone who could not manage on their earnings, must be spending their money selfishly. Parents who protested that they could not afford to buy adequate food were not believed.
>
> Meanwhile, in York, Benjamin Seebohm Rowntree, a member of the confectionery dynasty, was investigating the living conditions of thousands of poor families in the city. In 1899, he provided irrefutable proof of the poverty line, which bore out what some parents had said in court, that their wages were too low to provide even a frugal lifestyle for the family.
>
> Child neglect in the 1890s is just one of many subjects where mistakes could be made from using newspaper reports in isolation.

Detail

The amount of detail in newspapers can be a problem, if a researcher becomes side-tracked by it and fails to see the bigger picture.

Error

Newspapers are especially prone to errors of fact because of the number of times information was processed before it was finally printed. A reporter might not know that an interviewee had given wrong information, or that there was more to be had. He could have misheard something in a noisy courtroom if the acoustics were poor, or if there was shouting from the public gallery. With a tight deadline to write a report for his editor, he could accidentally have omitted a relevant detail. One of the telegraph operators transmitting or receiving his copy could have mistaken an important word. At the newspaper office, the report might have been shortened to fit into the space available, perhaps changing the meaning. Like the telegraph operator, the compositor typesetting the page could have made a mistake. The story that appeared in print may not reflect what had happened.

Many errors in newspapers are not serious differences but niggling inaccuracies that can be identified by checking more than one report, though this is not possible when there is only one source. There were comparatively few eighteenth century newspapers and perhaps only one of them included the story. Well into the nineteenth century, a sole contributor would supply identical copy to several editors, all of whom reproduced it verbatim. Later, news agencies supplied editors with the same information. Newspapers in the same group regularly used identical copy in all their titles. Sometimes a paper copied an interesting story from another publication. When there is only one source for a report, irrespective of the number of papers it can be found in, the researcher must judge whether it is reliable.

When two accounts that were written by different people agree about facts, those facts are likely to be accurate but, when practical, checking three independent accounts is advisable. When there is any discrepancy, checking several accounts is necessary to establish where consensus exists and what is in dispute. Sometimes credence can be given to a report that is not corroborated but a researcher who takes this course should have a good reason for doing so if it conflicts with anything else.

When using contentious information from a newspaper, check future editions to ensure that it is correct. Newspapers were sometimes sued for libel for running a false story. People who felt maligned by a newspaper report may have written to refute what had been alleged and sometimes a clarification was published.

Example

At the York Assizes, an action was brought by a young lady against a gentleman for a breach of promise of marriage; and as there is something singular in the contract which has been signed by the parties, we give it to our readers verbatim. "As love is the sublimest of passion, and has been the universal conqueror of mankind, we are not ashamed to own its influence, and do hereby agree to unite our hands and hearts in the silken bands of matrimony. As witness our hands"
    The jury found for the plaintiff with £200 damages.

Bath Chronicle and Weekly Gazette 15th April 1790
Derby Mercury 1st April 1790
Stamford Mercury 9th April 1790

At the assizes for a Northern County a young lady brought an action of damages against a young gentleman for a breach of promise of marriage. The jury found a verdict for the young lady with £200. The contract on which the action was grounded had the following emphatical expression. "As love is the sublimest of passion, and has been the universal conqueror of mankind, we are not ashamed to own its influence, and do hereby agree to unite our hands and hearts in the silken bands of matrimony."

Salisbury and Winchester Journal 20th August 1804
Bury and Norwich Post 22th August 1804
Royal Cornwall Gazette 25th August 1804

These two reports published fourteen years apart but referring to the same case, show why it is important to check information.

Fragmentation

Newspaper reports are usually brief and it is rare for the first report a researcher checks to provide the full story. When events unfolded over a period of time, it is necessary to read reports for successive days to discover what happened and perhaps several different publications need to be consulted to gain a rounded picture. Reading through short articles can take more time than envisaged because newspapers may not present information in a logical order for the researcher.

Electronic searching often locates several papers that contain a story. As reports tend to include very similar factual information, it is wise to prioritise the ones that seem most likely to yield meaningful results and check them first, only moving on to other publications if gaps or uncertainties remain.

Language

Very early newspapers can seem confusing to a new reader because of the writing conventions of the time. Until the early-nineteenth century the letter 's' was written as 'f' and nouns began with a capital letter. Verbs sometimes changed their ending in the way some European languages do. The meaning of some words has changed over time, whilst others are archaic and may not be in a modern researcher's vocabulary.

Legibility

Scanned newspapers are usually very small when they arrive on the computer screen which means resizing to make them large enough to read. Not all newspapers have survived in good condition and the scans made from poor quality originals may be difficult to read. On occasions, the scanning software has not translated words or figures accurately.

There are particular problems with very old newspapers as they rarely had headlines, the print size was small and a copious amount of information may have been crammed into a very small space. Electronic search facilities can locate the approximate position of the item on the page, but the researcher may still have to read through plenty of other material before finding the section that is wanted.

Neither language nor legibility are insurmountable problems but they can mean that research will take longer than hoped or envisaged. This should be factored into any plan when time is a critical factor.

Negativity and Sensation

Newspapers include plenty of heart-warming stories but much of what they printed prominently focussed on the negative. A journalist could find plenty to fill the newspaper columns by sitting in the local court house for a day taking notes, so it is far easier to research a man who had a brush or two with the law than his neighbour who lived a blameless life. Some newspapers made a point of seeking the bizarre and the scandalous and presenting it in a sensational manner. As a result, newspapers often record deviations from the expected norms of conduct, rather than how most people actually lived, making it seem that life in the past was more colourful than it actually was. Considering whether an incident was a frequent occurrence or a freak one is the best way of guarding against the false impressions that could arise from sensational content.

Satire and stereotype

Newspapers reported for a readership that was conversant with the values and issues of the time and the conventions of its journalism. Satire has flourished from the eighteenth century through to the twenty-first and can be a trap for an unwary researcher. Newspapers generally reported in a factual manner but several took a satirical approach to some topics, particularly in the eighteenth century. The hallmark of satirical writing is that it deliberately makes its subject look ridiculous, by holding up its follies and vices to public ridicule. Techniques include nicknames, exaggeration, sarcasm and placing the person in improbable situations.

Satire is easy to identify in magazines such as *Punch*, which regularly use this style to make a point and it is also easy to spot in cartoons. It may be readily apparent that an acerbic piece about a famous public figure is satirical but it pays to be cautious with detail about someone who is otherwise unknown. This is especially the case with reports from the eighteenth century when satire was at its peak. If detail in a report seems at all doubtful, check a different newspaper.

Stereotypes in reporting can also be an issue. Mentally ill people and those with a learning disability or physical handicap were once regarded as legitimate figures of fun. In the eighteenth and nineteenth centuries, there are also many examples of women who received very vicious coverage, particularly in situations where they were standing up for their rights.

Selectivity

It is not feasible for a journalist to record every scrap of information about a piece of news and when putting an account together for a reader, it is essential that the narrative is coherent and covers the main issues. This means that journalists and editors have to select which facts to include and what to omit. Sometimes two newspapers present a very different account of the same piece of news, simply because of the facts they chose to include. Although individual newspapers can yield a great deal of information, they cannot be relied on to reveal the whole story.

Superficiality

Research that relies solely on newspapers and ignores other sources risks being superficial. Although electronic searching has made it possible to locate a wealth of relevant material quickly, this may not yield the complete picture. Newspapers may not identify the antecedents to an issue and they rarely evaluate the impact of an event after it has dropped out of the news. A rounded piece of research may need additional sources.

Conclusion

There is plenty to consider when planning to use newspaper sources and some of their strengths and weaknesses are opposite sides of the same coin. Whether a piece of research is good or indifferent will owe more to the researcher's approach than to the material itself.

Chapter 5

Issues that affect all Types of Source

In addition to the specific problems that affect newspaper sources, there are issues with all historical sources which a newspaper researcher must take into account.

Bias

Bias is present in almost every historical source. Individuals have their own value base and views, which are likely to colour their writing, especially when there are judgements to be made, or they are dealing with opinions rather than facts. Some writers manage to adopt a fair and balanced approach to their subject and consider the pros and cons of a situation in an even-handed way, before forming a conclusion based on the evidence available to them. Others are blatantly partisan from the outset, openly promoting one point of view and dismissing everything else as irrelevant, misguided or wrong.

Bias only causes difficulty when it has not been detected, as it can seduce an unwary reader into drawing wrong conclusions. Biased sources are not invalid, but a researcher needs to decide how much of it can be relied on, and for what purpose. A balanced, objective piece of journalism does not necessarily make interesting reading or provoke debate, and opinionated contributors may have been commissioned because they had a partisan approach to their subject.

Cultural bias

Cultural bias occurs when a source reflects the values that are held by a particular group of people. Newspapers were very susceptible to this because they were private businesses trying to make money by attracting regular readers. One of the best ways of securing repeat custom was to appeal to certain points of view and to present news reports and opinion pieces that resonated with people who held those beliefs. Content that challenged the regular reader's preconceptions and prejudices was less likely to be included in that paper.

> **Example**
>
> When workers began to fight for better rights in the nineteenth century, employers who feared that such change would damage their own interests did not want to read that their workers had a valid point. They preferred reassurance that change would have undesirable consequences and should be resisted at all costs.

Even if some newspaper content is biased, it does not follow that everything it includes is tainted. The paper may only have been interested in steering opinion on certain subjects and may have had a balanced approach in the rest of its reporting.

Although cultural bias can be discerned in individual publications, it is easy for a researcher to avoid being misled. Newspapers have always catered for diverse audiences with different views. By checking publications that were not under the same ownership, a researcher should be able to isolate the effects of this form of bias within any single title.

Individual Bias

Individual bias occurs when a person is able to promote their own view rather than reflect on the situation objectively. A newspaper's contributors, editor and proprietor were all in a position to put their own slant on a report. The journalist's capacity to influence was the most limited, as his copy could be changed by someone more senior in the newspaper hierarchy, but most news desks worked to a tight schedule and it was probable that the reporter's account of any routine situation, if well written, would find its way into print. Journalists were skilled writers, who knew how a careful choice of words could be used to create a desired perception in a reader's mind.

> **Example**
>
> An explorer who ignores all risks in pursuit of a goal, might be described as brave, determined, foolhardy or stubborn, depending on the writer's viewpoint. A woman standing trial for theft could be presented as someone who was motivated by greed, made desperate by hunger or the hapless victim of coercion.

In addition to the power of language, editors also had the power of persuasion and the power of selection available to them. The daily editorial allowed the editor to express a view on any aspect of the news that captured his attention and to promote or decry the views of others. The power of selection gave the editor the right to decide what news went into the paper and how it was presented.

Proprietors, by virtue of the capital they provided, were also in a position to dictate the content and presentation of the news and editorial. The press barons of the early twentieth century took full advantage of this right.

Detecting Bias

Bias presents its biggest challenge when it is covert or hidden. Whilst cultural bias is hard to disguise, individual bias may be more difficult to detect as it can involve techniques such as deliberately falsifying information, misinterpreting facts, trying to portray opinion as fact, or selecting the facts which create a desired impression. This is another reason for checking more than one source before accepting that a piece of journalism is accurate. An unexpectedly brief report, or one that focuses on a surprisingly narrow element of a story is always worth verifying. The brevity was probably no more sinister than multiple stories jostling for space but the newspaper, or one of its contributors, could have had an undisclosed agenda.

Example

In 1819, *The Times* gave relatively brief coverage to a claim for damages by Maria Spenser after her former fiancé made an unfounded accusation about her morals in a public house. *The Manchester Guardian* was not sympathetic to her and reported much more detail, revealing that the defamation consisted of one indiscreet comment to Maria's brother-in-law in a private room by a tipsy man who quickly retracted his words. The only reason the accusation became public was because Maria's brother-in-law repeated the remarks to several of his customers. Readers of *The Times* saw a maligned young woman who deservedly avenged her honour in court with large damages. *The Manchester Guardian*'s readers were confronted with an opportunistic minx whose family manipulated a situation for financial gain.

There are other symptoms which should lead a researcher to consider whether a source is partisan. Unduly emotive or intemperate language, focussing on just one side of a story or summarily dismissing an alternative viewpoint, gaps in coverage and leaving questions unanswered may all be signs of a biased approach.

It is unusual for all the news about a person, cause or social group to be either very positive or invariably negative. When this is the case, consider whether the newspaper may have been trying to influence wider opinion rather than providing an objective view.

Example

By the 1860s, *The Times* had developed an aversion to breach of promise claims, considering that awards of high damages unfairly enriched undeserving women. There are periods when the cases it reported in detail were ones which supported its stance. Cases where a woman had been badly treated and deserved substantial compensation tended to be dealt with more briefly, or not reported at all.

Just because a newspaper had a partisan approach to a subject does not mean that it always adhered to this. A new editor or proprietor could lead to a change in the paper's attitude, as could a change in the situation itself or in the wider public mood.

Managing Bias

The best way to manage bias is not to rely on just one newspaper in isolation, however respected and authoritative. By consulting a selection of publications the bias in any individual paper should become apparent and one of the other newspapers, perhaps equally biased in the opposite direction, may well carry the counter-argument, enabling a researcher to come to a more perceptive conclusion.

> **Example**
>
> A balanced study relating to relations between Ireland and Britain in the late-nineteenth century would include a couple of national newspapers published in England alongside a couple of important newspapers from Ireland. Further depth could be added by careful selection of some local newspapers from both countries, perhaps one from an area that became part of the Republic of Ireland and one from the six counties that became Northern Ireland. A paper that served Liverpool, where there was a large immigrant Irish population, would be valuable also, as would one published in Scotland. Choosing a further area of England that did not have strong connections with Ireland could indicate how prevalent the views being expressed by national English newspapers really were.

Censorship

Censorship involves the use of power or authority to prevent information being published. It is especially evident in wartime, and in the conflicts of 1914–18 and 1939–45, draconian laws compelled British newspapers to follow an approved line in their reporting. This was to avoid giving any help to the enemy, as the telephone and telegraph had made communication almost instantaneous. Censorship was also designed to maintain public morale and support for the war effort amongst the civilian population.

Restrictions extended far beyond the conduct or progress of military campaigns but their boundary was not defined. It was impossible to know where the authorities would draw the line if an editor was required to explain why a piece of news had been circulated, and, as anyone breaching the Defence of the Realm Acts could be tried by a military court, newspapers opted to err on the side of caution. The influence of censorship can be seen in the reporting of a rail tragedy that occurred in 1915.

Example

At Quintinshill in May 1915, a crash involving three trains caused the deaths of 246 passengers. The majority were soldiers bound for the battlefields. This was the worst ever loss of life on Britain's railways but the appalling carnage was barely noted by the press other than in newspapers that served Scotland where the tragedy had taken place. Whether people in England and Wales learned of the disaster depended on whether they saw one of the papers that published the news south of the border. Even amongst the papers that included the story, reporting was brief and muted, especially when compared with coverage of peacetime accidents on the railways or mining disasters that had resulted in a large number of deaths.

Many researchers accept that sometimes there are valid reasons for newspapers not to publish a story, or to omit certain information. In the twentieth century, official censorship muzzled the press in respect of certain types of news. The Official Secrets Act forbade information that might compromise national security from being revealed. Victims of sexual assault were given statutory anonymity. Juveniles who were involved in crime could not be identified after 1933, unless the court agreed that their name should be made public. Details about children or vulnerable adults who are the subject of any legal proceedings cannot necessarily be published. Court injunctions are available to organisations and private individuals to stop the press revealing detail that has been obtained unlawfully, is in dispute, or could cause harm.

Unlike bias, checking a number of newspapers will not lead to officially censored information being located. Editors who publish in defiance of the law would make themselves personally liable to criminal proceedings, a very effective sanction.

Whilst official censorship may curtail the content of a newspaper, a more challenging problem for a researcher is when unofficial influence has been exerted to guide the press, because there is probably no evidence that it happened.

Example

By 1828, newspapers regularly printed extracts from embarrassing correspondence that was read out in court. After hearing some compromising extracts from an old man's letters, a judge addressed the reporters who were in court and expressed the hope that the defendant's foolish words would not be published. A few newspapers mentioned the judge's request and gave a brief summary but no direct quotations. Most who reported the case gave neither the judge's words nor any indication of what was in the letters.

There is no way of knowing whether it was unusual that the judge made this request or unusual that evidence of it appeared in print.

When unofficial pressure has been brought to bear on an editor it seems unlikely that a serious public matter could be suppressed completely for all time because this would involve managing a wider set of records. The practical effect of unofficial censorship may merely mean that there is no information in the newspapers of the day.

Propaganda

Propaganda denotes the dissemination of information, which may or may not be true, in order to guide the reader to a predetermined viewpoint. Like censorship, it was very common during wartime when a report may have been unduly positive to maintain morale, or unduly negative about the enemy, to stir up patriotic feeling. Not long after war broke out in 1914, and for its duration, British newspapers included reports about the Germans that ranged from preposterous accusations to unlikely incidents.

Example

Chocolates dropped by Hun Airmen during raids.
*   There is reliable evidence that besides dropping bombs, the Hun airmen have been throwing down chocolates containing poison.*

Daily Mirror 21st February 1918

Propaganda usually originates from a very organised source, though not necessarily an official one. During times of war, a government may be the driving force behind propaganda as it tries to keep public opinion supportive, despite the privations of conflict. At other times, interest groups ranging from political parties to businesses, may make statements or issue information that is designed to place their views or products in a good light, or to detract from their opponents. Propaganda can be very sophisticated because it may use facts, though selectively, to establish the truth of its position.

The biggest challenge for a researcher is covert propaganda. If a newspaper was not aware that a statement or briefing had been designed to create a particular impression it could publish something untrue in good faith. Until the mid-twentieth century, people were generally deferential to authority and the institutions of state, which gave officialdom the opportunity to mislead if this seemed necessary. There is no way of knowing how often deliberately untruthful information from an apparently reputable source has gone unchallenged or undetected.

As with bias, guarding against the misleading effect of propaganda in newspapers is possible by checking several sources. The number of newspapers and their different approaches makes it very unlikely that they would all emphasise the same points. If sources that would normally have a divergent approach take a similar one, it is sensible to consider why this is the case.

Conclusion

Bias, censorship and propaganda are important issues for all historians as they can lead to wrong conclusions. Although these factors may mean that some reports in a paper cannot be relied upon to reveal the full picture, it does not follow that everything in that paper is tainted or that it has no value as cultural history. The manner in which the press displayed its bias across the centuries, or reported stories during times of censorship, are historical studies in their own right.

Chapter 6

Preparing to Research

As millions of newspaper articles are now available with a few clicks of a mouse, a researcher needs confidence, focus and discipline to get the best out of this rapidly growing source. Anyone who has not used old newspapers before might initially feel overwhelmed by the number of matches produced by a search, or become distracted by the other stories on the page. Historians who are new to newspaper research, or who are about to study an unfamiliar period, may choose to set a short session aside to work any natural curiosity out of their system. This is not wasting time because it will highlight what was important to the literate public of the age and how a newspaper of the period was set out. Good background knowledge of the period and its newspapers pays dividends when researching a specific topic, as it should help to identify which type of article to concentrate on first and where they are likely to be found in the newspaper. It may even suggest a subject to investigate.

What to research

Deciding what to research may be clear-cut. The only choice many family historians will have to make is which ancestor's life-story to pursue first. Anyone who makes an income from research and writing may have a defined commission to fulfil, whilst amateur historians will probably have strong personal interests that they want to develop and possibly present to an audience.

Some researchers will be undertaking a study involving newspapers as part of a qualification. Anyone in this position could usefully spend some time looking at old newspapers to discover what type of information is available before finalising their choice of project. Digitised newspapers are making it possible to investigate previously neglected topics, or challenge accepted theories, so an unresearched subject, or a new approach, may spring off the pages.

High quality research involves much more than finding a few articles about something that happened in the past. This is especially true now that digitisation has made newspapers very easy to search and it is unlikely that much credit will be available for reproducing or paraphrasing old copy. The best investigations are those that involve a range of historian's skills such as locating relevant information, analysing or critiquing it, setting it in context, combining several articles to build up a picture, forming hypotheses and conclusions, or using evidence from newspapers to illustrate or challenge a line of thought about the past.

Similar considerations apply to any story that the researcher hopes to sell as a book or magazine feature. As many people now read old newspapers for themselves and some post interesting finds on web-sites, any paid outlet for material that merely rewrites old stories in modern language, rather than placing them in some context or adding something new, may be very limited.

Time Considerations

Unless research is for private interest, time may constrain what can be achieved. Most research involves more than merely locating and recording information. Understanding it, and writing it up in a suitable manner for someone else to read, are also necessary. There are no rules about how long to allocate to each element. A researcher has to decide this on a case by case basis.

One risk when using newspaper sources is of spending too much time collecting information. It is easy to overestimate how many articles can be read in a research session, particularly if that session is of fixed duration. When there are small gaps in a report, beware of wasting effort by chasing peripheral detail, instead of focussing on the study as a whole. Sometimes several promising lines of enquiry emerge and a piece of research can broaden out beyond what was initially envisaged. If this is the case, it may be better to include a note of the further work that would add value in the project report, rather than try to cram too much into the time available, or produce something wide-ranging but superficial. Locating copious amounts of information, and not leaving enough time to draw out relevant learning, is usually less satisfactory than obtaining a smaller amount of data, understanding it thoroughly, placing it in a wider context and indicating how the research could be developed.

If the research has to be submitted to someone else, never underestimate the time that may be needed to write it up to an acceptable standard, especially if a deadline is involved, a word count has to be met, or conventions in presentation have to be adhered to. Few people can produce a flawless essay at the first attempt and citing sources can consume a surprising amount of time.

Hobby researchers are free to follow their interests as they choose but even where deadlines or word counts are not involved, an organised approach to searching for, recording and evaluating new discoveries will enrich research. When a change of direction or emphasis is warranted, taking a study to a suitable break point and keeping a note of what has been completed is always worthwhile. This makes it much easier to refer to this work at a later date, without wasting time backtracking.

Health and Safety

Not everyone who uses a computer is covered by health and safety legislation, as this depends on a person's employment status. Anyone who is engaged in on-line research will probably be using the same types of computer equipment as people who use them in their job. This means that they are subject to the same risks to their health and well-being that have been identified for paid staff who regularly use digital technology. Ignoring these risks, and the advice that has been issued by the Health and Safety Executive to minimise them, is foolish. The person who may suffer the long-term consequences is the researcher.

Repetitive Strain Injury, sometimes known as Work Related Upper Limb Disorders, can affect the neck, shoulders, arms, hands and fingers. This type of injury is caused by repetitive movements, such as the repeated striking of keys on a keyboard, or the clicking of a mouse. Typical symptoms include, but are not limited to, aches, swelling, tingling and painful movement. Left untreated, permanent damage may result.

Aches and pains affecting various parts of the body can also result from a poor working posture. This can be an especial risk for anyone who is not working in a formal environment. Offices, libraries and archives normally have workstations available but in informal settings it is easy to slip into bad habits. Home-based researchers who are planning to spend time online need a work place, whether temporary of permanent, where their computer can be positioned well. Using an office chair that is correctly adjusted also helps to promote good working posture.

In addition to musculo-skeletal problems, tired or strained eyes and headaches can result from protracted viewing of a computer screen.

The Health and Safety Executive has issued guidance about the use of display screen equipment and recommends taking adequate breaks from computer work. It suggests that regular, short breaks are likely to be more satisfactory than occasional longer breaks; a five-ten minute break after fifty-sixty minutes continuous screen and/or keyboard work is likely to be better than a fifteen minute break every two hours.

On-line viewing of old newspapers will probably not be a brief activity, so a researcher needs to plan a schedule which builds in regular breaks. No matter how much material needs to be found and studied, protective breaks are never a waste of valuable time. Apart from the possible damage to health, anyone who feels tired or achy, or whose concentration slackens, will not be working productively and is liable to make silly mistakes, or miss something important.

Advice about any persistent or recurring symptoms, or anything that seems unusual, should be sought as soon as possible from someone who is professionally competent to deal with the matter. Never assume that a problem will get better of its own accord, or that it can be worked through, or that other people would not make a fuss. Ignoring any warning signs can lead to something much more serious.

Equipment

If digitised newspapers are to be used well, the IT equipment used to access them needs to be suitable. Foremost is a good sized computer screen and, in practice, this may mean a laptop or a desktop computer. Any device with a small screen is very hard to work with, even if it does display the text clearly, because newspaper pages were very large, relative to most other printed sources. Even when a large screen is used, it may be necessary to magnify the page to make the text large enough to read and then scroll around the screen to find the article. If the text has not scanned well, a large amount of magnification may be needed.

Resizing text, scrolling around a screen and taking notes are all likely to be involved with newspaper research. Crouching over a low table, balancing a laptop on the knees, or resting it on a soft surface is not conducive to good quality work. Working from a firm surface that has enough room for the computer and for note-taking, should boost productivity.

Recording Information

There are several ways of recording information, none intrinsically better than another. The best approach for any researcher is to develop a method of note-taking that they are comfortable with. Some libraries and archives will permit a computer powered by its own battery to be used on-site and may allow a source to be photographed. Others may only be prepared to provide a printed copy of an article for a charge. It is the provider's right to decide how material can be recorded and it may be that the traditional method of paper and pencil is the only one available.

One feature of newspapers is that the individual articles tend to be short in comparison with many other printed sources and it may be necessary to consult several separate pieces. Making notes from a series of short reports can be slower and more disjointed than using longer texts and it is surprisingly easy to forget about recording the source when moving from one article to another. A researcher needs to take especial care with this as backtracking through several pieces can be time-consuming if the information needs to be located again.

Newspapers were packed with detail and it is possible to take too many notes, especially in the early part of a study when it may not be clear how relevant a fact will be. Before starting to research in earnest, decide what is the aim of the study, and how to strike a balance between collecting what is important and not becoming overwhelmed by unnecessary detail or peripheral information. Rather than taking notes, it may be possible to print out the article concerned to refer to later but if several are needed, managing the paper copies becomes an issue and the cost can quickly mount up if they have to be bought from the institution.

Some on-line providers allow a registered user to set up a research folder to save relevant pages for future reference. This enables material to be located and collected as one process and analysed on a separate occasion, which can be an effective use of time. It can also assist a researcher not to waste effort making notes about unnecessary points, reduce transcription errors and simplify rechecking source material if this becomes necessary. A disadvantage is the temptation to suspend critical judgement and save everything 'just in case', which only defers the task of deciding what is relevant.

There are some potential problems with saving to an on-line folder. It may not be possible to save any files from a library network at all and a printed copy may have to be bought from the archive. When material has been saved, the researcher will need to be logged in to the provider's site in order to look at the pages in their folder, which requires an internet connection and a password unless they visit the library again. Public libraries usually allow a member to register for on-line access so that they can view their folder from home.

As an alternative method of electronic storage, some providers allow a subscriber to download and save a scan of a newspaper page or article on the user's own computer. Downloads are often images that are provided as a Portable Document Format (PDF) file. Once downloaded, these scanned pages may not be searchable and a user may have to look through the whole page to locate their information.

Researchers who save pages to an on-line folder need to manage them in line with the service provider's routines. Anyone who downloads files to their own computer must be very disciplined about organising them and should immediately develop their own procedures for filing and naming.

Left unmanaged, the benefit of electronic storage may be lost, as surprisingly little time needs to pass before the precise reason for downloading an item becomes elusive. Before starting any on-line research it is wise to set up at least one computer folder for filing all material which is downloaded in that session. At the end of the session, at a minimum, transfer all the downloaded material to this folder and name the folder. Using the date for this purpose may be useful and has the advantage of keeping all the session's material together. If there is time available, consider whether to tag any or all of the files in the folder with a brief description or a note of the optimum reading order. PDFs downloaded from *The British Newspaper Archive* have a twenty-three digit reference number which is not useful for locating something in a hurry.

Conclusion

When old newspapers beckon, any time spent on mundane matters can seem like an irrelevant distraction but a little forethought usually improves the productivity of research sessions and pays dividends by saving time at a later stage of the project.

Chapter 7

Which Newspapers to Start With?

Most people only have limited time to devote to any research, so it is wise to make that time as productive as possible. This begins with the decision about which newspapers to consult first and being able to hone in easily on the titles and editions that may contain the most useful information is an important skill. It is exasperating to spend a few hours struggling to piece together a jigsaw through the pages of a dozen papers, only to find that the final one contains the full picture and more. De-motivation can soon set in when nothing from an initial search seems relevant, or if it produces no insight into the subject.

It is rare for reporting of any subject to be confined to just one newspaper and there are substantial overlaps between the content of national, regional and local versions. However, the different types of publication often give the same news a different emphasis, which makes some a better starting point than others. National papers are excellent for information about matters of countrywide significance, whilst regional and local ones tend to concentrate on the impact for individual places. When a local event, such as a disaster or accident, was important enough to be reported in national newspapers, material from the local newspapers is usually more detailed and informative. Beginning a study by prioritising a few selected titles can provide useful early insight. If the first articles do not yield enough good quality information, or if they demonstrate a need to look further, a researcher can easily refocus, or expand their investigation to other papers.

When researching from national newspapers, it can be tempting to restrict investigation to *The Times* and *The Guardian* which can be accessed for free, especially if time is at a premium. This would exclude *The Morning Chronicle* and *The Morning Post* which were both influential in their day and some twentieth century titles that may have addressed the issue in a different manner.

As there are already millions of newspaper pages on-line, and the number is growing by the month, the best way to find out what is available is an authoritative on-line source. *The British Newspaper Archive* has up-to-date lists of the titles it has digitised and the dates they cover. The *British Library* has detailed information about all newspapers, magazines and periodicals including those that are only available in print format.

Constitutional and Political History

National newspapers are a very good source for information about how the country was governed and its relationship with the rest of the world. At the top of the constitutional pyramid was the monarch and, until the early twentieth century, most national titles contained detailed coverage of royal lives and events. This extended to minor royalty as well as the reigning monarch and their immediate family.

Below the monarch came the Parliament and government. National newspapers reported the high profile speeches and debates on contentious topics that were discussed in the House of Lords and the House of Commons, alongside the routine minutiae of day-to-day parliamentary business. The activities of important politicians and peers, and sometimes of their families, were also noted.

Reports from the law courts also received wide coverage. As well as reports about high profile criminal and civil trials which would have appealed to readers craving sensationalism, the decisions taken by senior judges in the Courts of Appeal were covered in minute detail, perhaps with each judge's speech captured word for word. The reasons why judges decided a civil case in the manner they did, could be more newsworthy than the case itself. In nineteenth century Britain, several branches of law developed rapidly as senior judges established how legislation passed by Parliament should be interpreted, or reshaped the boundaries of existing legal practice, to take account of the reality of life and business dealings in a modern, industrialised society. Entrepreneurs and their advisors needed to keep up-to-date with the exact legal position and newspapers provided the information they required.

The best starting point for information relating to local government and politics is the local and regional newspapers for the place in question. Most literate people were very engaged with local affairs, in part because they were wealthy enough to pay the local rates that financed the many boards and committees tasked with running early public services. The proceedings of

Boards of Guardians, Boards of Health, Sanitary Committees, Local Education Committees and Council meetings are reported in enough detail to build up an informative picture of a place at a specific point, and to track changes in local services and public attitudes over time. Chartism, the working man's political movement of the 1830s and 1840s, the rise of the Labour movement in the late-nineteenth century and the demise of Liberalism as a nationwide political force in the early-twentieth century, were very well recorded in local newspapers, enabling the progress of change to be investigated on a place by place basis.

Economic History

Although all types of newspaper included economic news, and perhaps data from the commodity exchanges which operated in several major cities, titles that served a region or a large town have much to offer a researcher who wants in-depth understanding of economic matters. When Britain transformed into an industrial economy in the eighteenth century, many of its varied industries developed their own regional heartlands as manufacturers found that some sites offered natural advantages for their product. Steel foundries were concentrated in Sheffield, cotton factories in Lancashire, woollen mills in West Yorkshire and pottery kilns in North Staffordshire. Coal was mined from Scotland to South Wales but, as the seams were of vastly different thickness and quality, this was effectively a number of regional industries rather than a truly national one.

Shipping, foreign trade and fishing thrived in many coastal towns and villages, and along navigable rivers but there were great differences between the vast maritime ports and hamlets that had a tiny harbour for a few local vessels. Agriculture was a nationwide enterprise carried out by many producers whose land ranged from large fertile estates to poor-soiled smallholdings but this too had strong regional characteristics and crops varied from animal husbandry to grains or root vegetables, depending on the terrain.

As a class, industrialists and traders were not indifferent to national politics, foreign news or what was happening in other areas of the country. Their primary concern though, was for detailed coverage of anything that might impact upon their own business interests. Regional newspapers served this type of reader by providing relevant commercial and industrial news, alongside any local or nationwide developments that might affect them.

National newspapers included plenty of economic information but their approach was more general, and they might only report a significant industrial or economic issue some time after its first symptoms were discussed in the relevant regional or local newspapers.

Social History

Directly and indirectly, newspapers contain a wealth of information about the society of the time. Insights into life in the eighteenth century are usually gleaned from the many individual reports those papers contain. In the nineteenth century, this type of evidence was joined by a different type of material that became known as investigative journalism. Rather than waiting for stories to emerge, individual publications began to research topics that interested them and published the results. Some of these studies were very influential. One of the most enduring investigations was commissioned by *The Morning Chronicle* in 1849 into the living conditions of the poor. Six knowledgeable journalists toured the country and interviewed people in a manner that was not dissimilar to that adopted by official government investigations into factory working and sanitation earlier in the decade. As a result, the paper printed some very powerful and insightful articles about what life was really like in both industrial and agricultural districts and in London. No study of conditions in mid-nineteenth century Britain would be complete without reference to this material. Similarly, a study of society in the 1880s that neglected to interrogate *The Pall Mall Gazette,* would miss the horrifying revelations about child procurement published in 1885.

As investigations became an accepted form of journalism, national, regional and local papers included articles that revealed an aspect of society at a point in time. They were not necessarily part of a campaign for change, they might not have considered the full picture and the writer might have had a personal viewpoint to present. Despite these potential limitations, the reports are very useful. Without the information they had collected it may now be impossible to discover, with such precision, what life was really like because this type of commentary would not have featured in the news reports of the day.

Rich detail about what life was like in any place is abundant in its local newspapers. Routine articles about people's activities, leisure interests and problems disclose much about how they lived and the values they cherished, as do the letters they wrote. A researcher may need to collate several reports to establish the situation if there is no direct information provided by an investigative feature or editorial.

Disputes heard in the civil courts provide excellent source material for social historians and those who are interested in a range of other topics, even when the conflict that took the parties to court now seems uninteresting or archaic. Local newspapers will probably provide the most detailed account as they had plenty of space to fill. If the case was mentioned by a national newspaper, the coverage may have been very brief. Editors had plenty of material competing for space and often opted to summarise several stories rather than include an in-depth report about one or two.

Example

The Times devoted a couple of short paragraphs to a libel case between two Northamptonshire builders which was heard at the Norfolk Assizes in 1871. Its sparse account revealed only that a Mr Gent had written that Messrs Cosford had "scamped the work". After failing to justify this in court, Gent agreed to apologise and pay ten guineas in damages for his ill-judged words rather than let the jury decide the figure.

The *Northampton Mercury* included a full report of the hearing. A century and a half later, the copious detail provides legal historians with evidence of how the court process operated in practice in mid-Victorian times. For architectural historians, it adds to understanding of how the building and construction industry functioned at that point. Social historians will find information about the way society perceived public reputation and the importance attached to an unblemished character. Family historians will discover plenty of detail about the way the plaintiff and the defendant behaved and glimpse the personality of their ancestor.

As a rule of thumb, newspapers for the place in question are likely to carry the most detailed account of a local story but this cannot be taken for granted. If one of the parties hailed from a different part of the country, a paper serving that area might also report it. Newspapers across the land regularly included titbits of news from afar if the editor thought it would interest readers, or if there was little other material to fill the pages. Occasionally, the best account appears in a paper that had no connection with the story. When the local account is brief, or leaves unanswered questions, it is always worth checking other papers published around that date. There may have been a very important local news story that week, making coverage of unconnected items shorter than expected.

Family History

Newspapers serving the areas where ancestors lived or worked are the best starting point for family historians. Very few people were mentioned in national newspapers, and even if they were, local titles remain the most likely to have the best information, or any human interest details. Browsing full editions of newspapers published in the place where an ancestor lived, can provide insight into what they may have known about the wider world, their living conditions and their cultural values.

Foreign History

National newspapers and very early regional newspapers are good sources for news from foreign countries and from the Empire. With more money available than publications with a small circulation, some newspapers were able to retain knowledgeable people who lived abroad to provide them with news, or commission journalists to travel abroad to research stories.

British newspapers did not provide full information about situations in other countries. It is necessary to consult papers from the country in question for that level of detail. What British newspapers do reveal, however, is how much British readers knew about what was happening abroad. This can be helpful in understanding public opinion.

Wartime History

Wars are closely linked to national politics, so national newspapers offer a good starting point for conflicts, battles, negotiations, military matters and the Government's use of emergency powers. Regional and local papers provide information about the impact of war upon daily life for people in their area.

Conclusion

Finding the best place to break into any piece of newspaper research can make the task more productive from the outset and should help to shape the research plan. As a user's experience of newspaper sources increases, so too does their knowledge of where could be a good place to begin.

Chapter 8

Finding Material in On-line Newspapers

W hen a newspaper is made available on-line, help with finding relevant information is available via a search facility. This uses details entered by the researcher to locate articles that meet the specified criteria. Whilst there is no guarantee that everything (or even anything) will be identified, being able to use the search page with confidence maximises the chances of success.

Individual service providers have created their own bespoke search pages. Although they are all performing the same function they vary in appearance so, when using one for the first time, it is worth making the effort to become familiar with how it is set out and what options are available. Some providers offer a basic search for straightforward queries and an advanced one which enables a confident researcher to construct very sophisticated searches. Capital letters and hyphenation are usually not needed in the search term.

Search pages usually have some notes from the provider containing useful tips for using the search functions. For anyone new to on-line searching, the guidance may seem very technical and perhaps complex. If this is the case, experiment with the search boxes to find some material and then read the help notes again. They will probably be much clearer after hands-on experience.

Time spent developing good search skills will soon pay dividends. A researcher who can locate relevant material quickly has more time to spend understanding it, or following the new leads it reveals. The best way to become confident with searching is to master an element at a time until using a range of tools becomes second nature. This should not be a long process.

The most useful skills to develop initially are how to use straightforward filters, fuzzy searching, keeping search terms together and using wild-cards.

Filters

When words are typed into the search box, it is likely that plenty of matches will be found. A filter is a technique for locating the most relevant matches among

A basic search page for straightforward queries. (*Screenshot from The British Newspaper Archive*)

them. It works by identifying material that falls into specified categories and ignoring anything else. Filters are very useful with search terms that produce many potential matches, such as 'John Smith' or 'Lancashire Assizes'.

The most usual filter allows matches to be restricted by date. Some search pages achieve this by a tick box that enables the date to be progressively refined to a single day. On other sites, the date range is set by typing into a 'start date' and an 'end date' box.

It is normally possible to filter by type of content, meaning that only certain types of material are matched, such as editorial, news, readers' letters, items with illustrations or advertisements. These filters are usually activated by a tick box.

Family historians may be particularly interested in matches from the place where their ancestors lived. When a site hosts more than one newspaper a search can usually be restricted by filters to named newspapers, or to a particular place.

Sites with advanced search facilities will enable a query to be more focussed as they allow a user to search several terms at the same time. This enables additional terms to be filtered into the search as well as filtering unwanted matches out.

There is more likelihood of finding material with a wide-ranging search and a search without filters can be more productive than one with several in place. If a search produces a large number of matches, apply filters one by one to

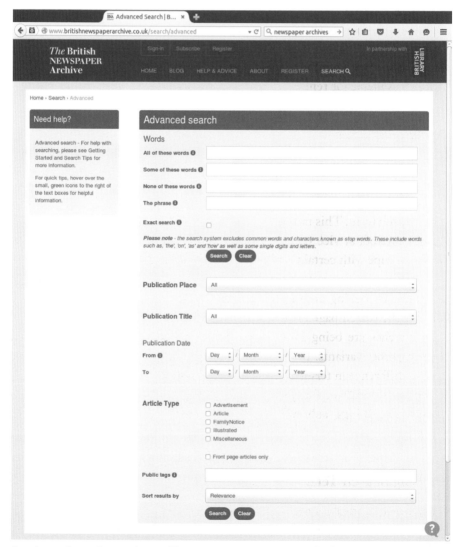

An advanced search page that enables a user to create a very sophisticated search. (*Screenshot from The British Newspaper Archive*)

focus in on those that seem to be the most relevant. If this does not produce any matches, remove any filter relating to place and try again. Occasionally, a story was reported in a paper from an unrelated part of the country, but not in the person's place of residence. If a short report about an ancestor is discovered in a local paper, remove any locality filters and restrict the date to a few weeks before and after the date of the report that has been found, in case a more detailed account is available in a paper that is not local.

Remember that some words and phrases were regularly used in advertisements and may return a very large number of irrelevant matches. When this happens, a category filter enables them to be excluded from the search. Reviews of the novel, *To Let* would be hard to spot amongst pages of advertisements for property available for rent.

Fuzzy Searching

As it is unlikely that a newspaper always used the exact words in the search term, multiple queries are needed to check for obvious variants. A fuzzy search can help with this, as it locates material that falls slightly outside the words used in the search term. This normally involves locating a plural noun when a single noun is entered, or vice versa, or a range of different verb endings. It may also be able to cope with certain types of mis-spellings and variable spellings.

Some search pages automatically use a fuzzy search, others require the user to set this by ticking an on-screen box. Before searching for material, check whether the search page normally uses an exact search or a fuzzy one. If only exact matches are being found, something important may be missed by not checking other variants. If a fuzzy search is being performed, related searches for tiny difference in terminology are not necessary.

Never assume that a fuzzy search will locate all possible variants of the search term. Mis-spellings, abbreviations and typological errors may lie outside its reach.

Keeping Search Terms Together

When a search involves a group of words, only reports that include the exact term may be of interest. The symbol " at the start and end of the search term will restrict matches to any that contain those exact words. If the symbol " is not used to open and close the term, the search may locate matches that contain all the relevant words but not as a phrase.

When the symbol " is not used, many sites will first list the results that use the precise term before moving onto ones where they occur separately.

Wild-cards

Wild-cards are a way of locating material that may not be found by a standard search. They work by replacing a letter or letters in the search term with a symbol. The most usual symbols are ? which normally replaces a single letter, and * which replaces more than one consecutive letter in a word. Before using a wild-card search, always check the provider's guidance to confirm which symbols they have used and what meaning they have given to them. Some sites have additional wild-cards which help to make searching even more sophisticated.

Wild-cards are helpful with words that were written with a variety of spellings over time. When the literacy level was low, there was often no consistency about which vowel was used in an a surname, or whether some of its consonants were double or single. Wild-cards are a more practical way of checking for variant spellings than manually trying every possible combination.

When searching for material that was published before 1830, use a wild-card to replace the letter 's', when typing in the search term. The letter 's' used to be denoted by a symbol that is very similar to the modern lower case 'f'. This usage declined between 1810-20. Some scanning software has interpreted the letter as 'f' and a query using 's' does not always return all results.

Conducting a Search

Common sense, a bit of knowledge of the period and lateral thinking all have a part to play in productive searching. Sometimes, typing words into a search box and seeing what emerges will produce relevant matches but working in an organised manner, thinking carefully about the words in a query, and using appropriate wild-cards, all maximise the likelihood of retrieving whatever information is available about a topic and not missing anything important. It is advisable to keep a record of all searches made to prevent time-wasting repetition. Sometimes, reviewing a list of searches that have been made may identify a gap or trigger further ideas.

Avoid Frequently Used Phrases

Try to avoid unduly general words and terms that are often used in everyday life, because they tend to produce a large number of matches that cannot be easily reduced to a manageable level by filters. If necessary, find out more information about the subject and incorporate this in the query. Search boxes labelled 'name' can be used for any word, not just a name.

Example

When searching for reviews of the novel *To Let*, find out the author and publication date. A query that includes the name of the author, John Galsworthy, and its publication date, 1921, has a much greater chance of producing relevant matches than one using only its title.

Language and Conventions

Search terms which use the language of the period have the best chance of success, because the way a subject is referred to now may have developed after the event. For example, the 'First World War' and 'World War One' are terms which originated well after the 1914-18 conflict, which was initially referred to as the 'Great War', or even just 'the war'.

The conventions of the time are also important. Well into the twentieth century, a married woman may have been described as Mrs followed by her husband's forename rather than by her own. Professional people were sometimes referred to by a job title such as Councillor, Doctor or Reverend rather than a forename.

Synonyms

Try replacing words in a query with ones which have the same meaning if the initial search does not produce many matches.

Phonetics

Think about the sound of a proper name and use a query which replicates this rather than concentrating on a usual spelling. A name that was written as heard, by a person who could not understand an accent, might be too different to be found by a fuzzy search or a wild-card. The family named Quillan may have been listed as Cullen, or the name Alison could have been recorded as Ellison.

Abbreviations and Initials

Some male forenames had a recognised abbreviation; Jas for James, Hy for Henry, Thos for Thomas and Wm for William are examples of this. Elizabeth was frequently altered to Betty or Bessy, Margaret to Peggy and Mary was often interchangeable with Polly. When there were a number of names in a list, such as those present at a meeting or awarded a school prize, an initial and surname may have been used instead of a forename.

Ignore Proper Names

When a query with a person's name does not produce the expected result, it is worth searching for the event without including a name. The newspaper may not have mentioned the person's name, or they could have been known by an alias. Oral history is not always accurate, and a tale handed down the generations might have specified the wrong person. A search for 'manslaughter' and 'Huddersfield' or 'runaway horse' and 'Preston' might produce a positive result.

Browse some Editions

If an approximate date is known, browsing newspapers published around that time may be helpful. Something as simple as a typesetting error may account for the failure of a search. Browsing may be the most practical way of finding material about the antecedents of an event or incident. It may even identify a contemporary search term that would locate relevant material.

Extend the Time Frame

Newspapers occasionally revisit a story, perhaps as part of an anniversary. There may have been an article that reappraised an event with the benefit of hindsight, or in context of changed public opinion. There could even have been an interview with someone mentioned in the original account which gives a different perspective or additional information. Suffragettes, who were vilified by the press before 1914 for demanding votes for women, were interviewed many years later and received coverage which was understanding and often admiring. Retrospective material can add depth to a new study of a topic and can also prevent the frustration of researching a subject that has already been well-covered in the present era.

Search Again after some Time has Passed

There are plenty more newspapers to be digitised. If a provider is still adding new material, consider checking it again at a later date.

Deciding which Matches to Investigate

If a search produces a large amount of relevant material after all possible filters have been applied, it may be necessary to prioritise it. Sometimes, a quick glance at the list of matches will reveal those that are irrelevant. A footballer may have had the same name as an ancestor, or a topical phrase may have cropped up in the name of a racehorse. When this is the case, it should be possible to ignore any report from the sports pages.

The list of matches may be presented either in chronological order, or in an order that the search page considers the most useful. If the search page has tried to prioritise matches, it will list items where the words in a search term are all together before it presents those where the individual words are separated. The algorithm used to conduct searches is sophisticated and its suggestions of where to start are often sensible.

Decide what type of history the research study represents and then consider the points made in Chapter 7 about which papers are especially good for breaking into a topic of this type. It may be appropriate to begin with a few carefully selected titles.

If the list of matches contains a number of local or regional papers, try to establish which ones are likely to include an identical report. An evening paper for a town may contain exactly the same information as the next morning's edition.

The list of matches will probably show the opening words of the report. If several begin with exactly the same words, they probably originated from the same source. Some reports may contain a little more detail than others, depending on how the material was edited by different people. A researcher has to decide, in the context of their investigation, how much time they are prepared to spend checking every report when there are a large number.

Look at the quality of the opening words in any on-screen match. Newspapers in poor condition may not have not scanned well and the word preview they produce is muddled. Opt for the ones that give a good preview first. Those which may be in bad condition can be checked later, if necessary.

How to be sure a report is the right one

It can be hard to identify people who are not well-known from newspaper reports alone, if there is not much personal detail. In many cases, a historian will have to use other knowledge to decide whether the report is relevant. This may not be straightforward, because an unusual name may have been well-used within a family, making it impossible to know whether the bearer was a direct ancestor, or a distant cousin. Age is not necessarily helpful, because people were often hazy about this until the twentieth century.

Distressing Finds

The past was not a pretty place, and anyone who makes a study of old newspapers is bound to come across some material they find distressing. Family historians may discover an ancestor who committed an appalling crime, or who was harshly punished for what now seems a trivial misdemeanour. If a relative was involved in an accident, the account may include horrific detail that would probably not find its way into print today. Newspapers were not always reticent about naming the victims of serious assaults which can be upsetting for descendants, especially if they can remember the person.

Family historians are not the only researchers who might be upset by what they discover and it is not unusual for any reader of old newspapers to feel emotions ranging from grief to anger when first encountering a story. Journalistic styles have changed over time and the reporting of industrial disasters can be painful in its poignancy. Public tastes have also changed. In the nineteenth century, there was a macabre fascination with how condemned prisoners spent their final hours or met their end. There are reports of accidents that could have been foreseen and prevented by an employer and of degrading or inhumane treatment meted out to people whose only fault was that they could not support themselves and their families. A few reports seem to indicate a miscarriage of justice, or a cover-up, or the deliberate scape-goating of someone who was too poor or uneducated to defend their own position.

Old newspaper reports can cause distress to living people, by revealing something they hoped was buried in the past. Information in old newspapers is considered to be in the public domain but before electronic searching, it was probable that a shameful incident that happened over half a century ago would not become known to children, grandchildren, neighbours or friends. As life expectancy is substantially greater now than even a generation ago, news from the early twentieth century may still have the potential to hurt. Examples of news that some people may prefer to remain forgotten include a conviction for a minor crime in their youth, being involved in a fatal accident, even if no blame was apportioned to them, or being named in connection with a divorce suit.

Any researcher who discovers this type of information about someone who is still alive should think carefully before publicising it and, if necessary, take professional advice to ensure that no laws would be contravened by doing so. A criminal conviction in a person's youth may be covered by rehabilitation of offenders requirements and a victim of a sexual crime may now be protected by anonymity, even if their name was published at the time.

If the matter is not covered by law, there are moral issues when using information that could cause a person distress. This includes information about someone who is deceased if it could upset a close relative. Although society is much less censorious about how people conduct themselves than it was a few generations ago, there are some who would prefer a parent's, spouse's or sibling's flouting of convention to remain a secret, or who may have no knowledge that it ever happened. Once information has been disclosed to the person concerned, discussed with other members of the family, or posted on a website, it is impossible to revert to the status quo that once prevailed. The wisest course may be to maintain the secret until revealing it will not hurt anyone.

Conclusion

Although electronic searching offers no guarantees that every scrap of information will be found, the ability to construct specific queries often means that plenty of relevant material will be discovered. For some researchers, just finding and reading an old report or two may be sufficient for their purposes. For anyone interested in using old newspapers to investigate some aspect of history in detail, and perhaps make exciting new discoveries, their preserved pages contain plenty of information that will shed new light on the past.

Chapter 9

Historical Studies using Old Newspapers

Newspapers may be treated in the manner their original audience would have used: read through once and then put on one side. Historians can approach them in another way: extracting information from multiple editions for an in-depth investigation about an aspect of life in the past. A simple study could involve collating half a dozen reports to obtain a more detailed picture. A complex investigation might entail extracting and analysing data from a very large number of reports, to discover what was really happening behind the newspaper headlines, or over a period of time.

Collating Articles

The purpose of collating articles is to build up a more rounded account. Core elements of a story are usually the same in newspapers but the individual journalists who wrote reports tended to include different peripheral detail. Sometimes this reveals what a person was wearing, the actual words spoken and background information about the incident. Occasionally, a single reporter could capture a very precise detail that sparks the story into life, such as a young admirer tossing flowers to a convicted prisoner who was being led from the dock, or a generous neighbour offering his savings to a woman who had just been widowed by a dreadful industrial accident.

The first stage in building up a story from several accounts is to locate all the available material. Select the most detailed account and either print it out directly, or type it up and print it out so that it can be used as a work sheet.

Work through all the other accounts in turn, annotating the main report with any extra information, and the name and date of the paper or papers that included it. Record any contradictions between anything in the main report and any other in a similar manner.

When all accounts have been checked, review the main report and its annotations. Where there is only one source for any point, consider whether it is reasonable to accept this detail. If there are any contradictions in the evidence, decide which version is most probable and why. Make a note of the reasons for this decision as it can be difficult to recall the precise reason for any choice after a period of time.

Combine all the information on the work sheet into a single, chronological account and list all sources used, perhaps referencing pieces of information with footnotes. Check this through, ensuring that there are no inconsistencies.

Validating other Accounts

Newspapers can be helpful in verifying any sources that were written some time after an event. A book may have covered something in pared down detail, including only the most essential facts, or the account may have been written with the intention of creating a desired impression, rather than being wholly accurate. Memory is not reliable, especially after the passage of time and the memoirs of someone who did not keep a diary may have inadvertently placed incidents at the wrong time, or in the wrong town, or in the wrong order.

Work systematically through the source to check it, noting any discrepancies and anything which had been left out. Any differences or omissions will need to be corroborated by independently written reports in other newspapers in order to conclude that the account being validated was wrong.

In addition to checking what is in the source, it is worth searching newspapers to locate all mentions of the person or topic. If the source has not mentioned something relevant, valuable information might otherwise be missed.

Topic Studies

Newspapers contain plenty of information that can be aggregated to answer certain questions. Methodologies that were developed in social sciences investigations can be used in these studies. Some types of data are readily available and it is just a matter of working through the newspapers to extract it. Economic historians are very well-served by data such as commodity prices and weather information, which was printed daily.

Researchers who are interested in how an element of society functioned can also find plenty of data to analyse but they may need to apply a little thought and ingenuity when deciding what to collect. A newspaper may not always have provided information in a direct manner, making it necessary to infer the situation. Inference is a valid technique which involves making a logical deduction about something that is not known from information that is known. It is not the same as guessing, which is not a valid approach to a historical study.

Example

A newspaper reports that Miss Jones, one of Colonel Jones's two daughters, has been injured in a carriage accident and that her recently engaged sister has cut short a visit to her fiancé's family. If it is possible to discover which of Colonel Jones's daughters had just become engaged, the identity of the injured girl can be inferred.

If it is not possible to discover which of the sisters is newly engaged, then stating the identity of the injured girl would simply be a guess.

Another technique that a researcher may need to use is to find a proxy for a piece of information. A proxy is a piece of data that can be used as a substitute if something is not available. A proxy can never be infallible but well-chosen ones can provide valuable insight.

Example

Newspapers do not record a person's social class. They usually mention an occupation, which is an appropriate proxy.

Any topic study requires commitment, and the time and effort involved should never be under-estimated, but conscientious researchers should acquire a greater understanding of their subject than from just reading a few reports in isolation. There are two main approaches to structuring a topic investigation.

Case Studies

Case studies concentrate on individual experiences in order to understand a process or situation. The study involves analysing a number of examples of the same occurrence to draw out relevant learning. A case study restricts its conclusions to the examples it studies and does not attempt to generalise its findings to cover society as a whole. As case studies can be carried out with little or no use of numbers, researchers who are not confident with numbers might prefer this type of approach to one that seeks to quantify its findings or make generalisations from its results.

A case study can also be a wise choice when research time is restricted as it requires fewer examples to be located than a study that aims to draw conclusions about wider society.

Case studies can only be carried out when there is enough detail about each case to provide understanding. If newspapers only provided a few sketchy facts, there may not be enough material to investigate.

Choosing Examples for Case Studies

It is helpful to read about several cases before selecting the ones to study in depth and to pick ones that may provide breadth of learning. Newspapers covered the unusual in preference to the mundane, so settling for the first items located by a search may not lead to helpful conclusions. If the majority of cases being studied are unusually melodramatic, tragic or comical, rather than typical instances, they may give a completely false impression. Unusual cases do not have to be ignored because the reason why something was different may reinforce the conclusions that arise from the more usual ones.

An alternative approach to choosing the cases, if sufficient material is available and the number of cases is not excessive, is to look at all instances for a defined period of time or in a specific locality.

When creating case studies, be alert to what else was happening at the time. When newspapers had plenty of high profile events and campaigns to cover, routine news often struggled to find a slot. In these periods very determined searching may be needed to locate typical rather than unusual examples.

Quantitative Investigations

Quantitative investigations are more impersonal than case studies. They involve collecting and analysing information from many examples in a numerical manner, rather than focussing on individual experiences. They can provide good insights into how society functioned, though what a quantitative investigation identifies as a typical situation might not have been true of any of the items that are included in the study. With quantitative investigations it is important to use material which will yield valid conclusions and the best studies make the effort to find representative examples.

Hybrid Studies

Historical studies can combine the methodology of case studies and quantitative studies when investigating and presenting the findings. Case studies may present their conclusions in a numerical manner in order to draw out themes. Actual cases can be used to illustrate a quantitative study to give depth and context.

Choosing Examples for Quantitative Investigations

In many cases, it may not be practical, or even possible, to extract data from every example. In this situation, sampling is a technique that will provide good insight, provided that the sample is representative of the population it is drawn from and free from statistical bias. Samples drawn from newspapers can carry a strong risk of statistical bias because the papers were more likely to report unusual cases. As a consequence, some types of samples may contain a higher proportion of atypical examples than exists in the total number of cases.

If samples are selected in a manner to minimise statistical bias the conclusions drawn can be as meaningful as if all possible examples had been included. There are some statistical techniques for deriving as unbiased a sample as possible, which can be used when every item in the total population can be identified. Data that was recorded daily, such as commodity prices, can be sampled in this manner.

This type of sampling may not be feasible in some investigations because every item in the total population is not known. Although it is technically possible, it would be an enormous undertaking to find, and list, every example included in newspapers before any investigation work could begin. When this is the case, there are some methods of sampling which produce reasonable results if the sample size is large enough and effort is made to avoid obvious bias or distorting factors. Relying on the first examples located by a search is not one of them.

Cluster Sampling

This type of sampling involves focussing on an element such as a year, a month or a place and taking its examples from there. This approach does not have to be restricted to just one cluster, several can be used in conjunction to obtain a much larger number of items. If sampling covers a period of time, ensure there is nothing unusual about it that might affect data. December, for example, may not be a representative month because of Christmas. Similarly, March/ April and July/August can be affected because they were months when Assize courts were held. This could make them unrepresentative for some studies but an obvious source of data for others.

Quota Sampling

This provides a sample containing characteristics that might be expected to yield good information about a topic.

Example

A sample of 100 people who had brought a case in the civil courts might be structured as:

10 men aged 60+ years	10 women aged 60+ years
10 men aged 51-60 years	10 women aged 51- 60 years
10 men aged 41-50 years	10 women aged 41-50 years
10 men aged 31-40 years	10 women aged 31-40 years
10 men aged 21-30 years	10 women aged 21-30 years

The disadvantage with quota sampling is that the researcher has to prejudge what might be important when setting the quota and could, potentially, miss out on learning about other factors. It might also be difficult to find the right number of cases to fill some categories.

Stratified Sampling

If some of the characteristics of the population are known it may be possible to select samples that reflect these properties.

> **Example**
>
> If there were 1,000 court cases in a 4 year period, with 400 heard in 1851, 300 in 1852, 200 in 1853 and 100 in 1854, a set of samples could be weighted in the proportion 4:3:2:1 to represent this.

Sampling by Newspaper

As newspapers tended to cover the same material, it may be appropriate to draw the sample from a restricted set of newspapers, ensuring that the titles covered all areas of the country and appealed to different types of reader. When sampling by newspaper, ensure that some local or regional titles are included. National newspapers had plenty of material to choose from and are likely to have printed the more extreme cases rather than the routine ones. Local newspapers are most likely to contain the best detail.

Whatever methodology is used to obtain a sample, keep a record of why this was chosen and any assumptions that were made as this may need to be declared if the research is publicised in any way. Even if the selected sample is not obtained by a standard method, it may still provide good insight into a topic, confirm lines of enquiry and open up new ones. Samples can be extended and doing so may move a study to the point where it is possible to generalise its conclusions.

How Many Items Should be Included in a Sample?

If a quantitative study hopes to discover something about the total population, it must include enough examples. For most types of data, many statisticians agree that a sample must contain at least twenty items that were selected independently, before any general themes or conclusions can be drawn with confidence about the total population it represents. The more items that are included, the greater the likelihood that findings are not the result of chance and reflect the characteristics of the total population. Because of the practical problems of finding a statistically unbiased sample for some types of historical investigations, it will be necessary to err on the side of caution and include plenty of examples. A sample can never be too large but it can be too small and in practice, twenty is very unlikely to be adequate.

Studies which are general, or which span a long period, will need a much larger number of examples than ones which cover a short period, are restricted to a geographical area, or have a specific question to answer. If the researcher knows enough about the total population to apply the relevant formulas, there are some statistical techniques that can assist with working out the minimum size of the sample for the study in question. When it is not possible to calculate a number, the researcher will have to apply their own judgement, based on their existing knowledge of the subject and period.

Although there can never be too many items in a sample for statistical purposes, this is not the only aspect a researcher should consider when planning a study. How much data they can find, or handle, are both relevant. Well thought out investigations that contain an adequate number of items may reach better conclusions than one with many more examples if the researcher had to spend too long collecting the data, struggled to analyse it, or had no time to set the findings in context.

Coding

Historians who want to analyse situations, whether for a case study or a quantitative investigation, may find that it is cumbersome to deal with any aspects that are not normally expressed in numbers. Coding is a technique that allows a situation to be recorded in a very concise way, usually by assigning a letter or number to represent it. A code can be very simple, such as a Yes / No answer to an objective question such as whether or not someone is married. It can also be used to represent something more complex, even subjective, such as someone's social class or their motive for behaving in a particular way.

Example

Although people who brought claims for damages to court in the nineteenth century each had their individual reasons, there are themes that link them, such as compensation for a loss, revenge, fraud, or establishing their honour.
   This could be represented in code as:

Compensation	C
Revenge	R
Fraud	F
Honour	H

A researcher usually has to devise their own codes, striking a balance between being too general and too specific. There is plenty of diversity in historical situations and it may not be feasible to code every nuance, especially when a large number of cases is being studied. Sometimes, too many options in a code may make it hard to discern underlying patterns.

Often, simply assigning a letter or number to represent a situation will be sufficient. Codes that use a combination of letters and numbers can sometimes be helpful but may prove too cumbersome for anyone who does not already have some expertise or experience.

When codes are being devised, try to eliminate the potential for error by thinking carefully about what numbers or letters to use. Avoiding numbers as the only element in a code prevents any inadvertent confusion with numerical data in the study. If more than one aspect of a situation is being coded, not using the same letter more than once reduces the likelihood of making an error. Take care also when using the letter O and the number 0.

Coding comes into its own when data from an investigation is recorded and investigated electronically as it allows data to be sorted and grouped very quickly. Without coding it may not be possible to use electronic methods.

Conclusion

The purpose of any historical investigation is to obtain insight into an aspect of the past. It is not to collect data for its own sake or calculate a series of facts about it. When it is not possible to study every instance of an event, well thought out studies that collect and analyse a moderate quantity of data thoroughly can produce as good insight as a much larger sample.

One risk faced by newspaper researchers is that the incidents which received most coverage often had unusual features and did not reflect the situation as most people would have experienced it. The best learning is likely to occur when the researcher understands the typical and is able to place atypical examples in context.

Chapter 10

Some Data Handling Techniques

There are two main ways in which researchers benefit from being able to handle data. The first is that grouping and analysing can provide new insights into a topic and indicate areas where further investigation would be beneficial. The second is relevant to anyone who wishes to communicate their results to others. Numbers have a definite meaning that is missing from subjective terminology such as 'many', plenty' or 'a few' which people can understand in different ways. Good history needs evidence and numbers can provide certainty in a way that vague or imprecise expressions do not.

In the investigation and data collection phases of a project, researchers may develop a gut feeling about what the study will reveal. This is not always confirmed when the data is checked. It is surprising how often 'almost everything' turns out to be a measurement such as 80 per cent, 7/10 or 3/4. These are all high proportions that will give plenty of insight into the topic but a substantial minority of data does not have this attribute. If the other 20 per cent, 3/10 or 1/4 also share similar characteristics, concentrating on 'almost everything' probably means overlooking pertinent issues.

As well as providing a degree of exactitude, numbers are a useful way of presenting information visually. In some situations, the charts and graphs that can be produced from them convey information more clearly than a piece of written text.

Some people are not comfortable with using numbers but historical investigations are not like scientific and engineering subjects where calculating a precise number may be the difference between the success and failure of a project. Historical research does not involve computing or assigning a definite number to anything and, in most cases, striving for absolute precision would add nothing to informed understanding of the past. There is no benefit in trying to find out whether 23 per cent, 24 per cent or 26 per cent of a data set conform to a particular parameter. What is significant is that around a quarter of the items being studied have this feature and the questions this knowledge could trigger.

For example, was this quarter the smallest category in the analysis or was it the highest individual proportion of several other elements? What were those other elements? What might have caused the differences between them?

Confidence with just a few techniques can open up many new lines of enquiry about the past. Initially, the most useful ones for a historical researcher to be able to calculate and interpret are percentages and averages.

Percentages

Percentages, denoted by the sign %, express any number as a proportion of 100. This is a useful way of comparing numbers. Without this it would be difficult to say whether 29/83 is greater or less than 34/97 and, as a consequence, to reach meaningful conclusions.

In order to express a percentage, two numbers are needed. One is the total number of values in the data set – the denominator. The other is the total number of values in the data set that are relevant – the numerator.

To convert a number to a percentage, divide the numerator by the denominator and multiply the answer by 100. It is given by the formula:

$$\frac{\text{numerator}}{\text{denominator}} \times 100\%$$

Example

29/83 boys and 34/97 girls from a school passed the 11+ examination. Did the boys or girls perform better?

$$\frac{29}{83} \times 100\% = 34.9\%$$

$$\frac{34}{97} \times 100\% = 35.1\%$$

Converting both results to percentages demonstrates that the boys and girls performed almost the same.

As shown in this example, most calculations of percentages do not work out to a whole number and a researcher has to decide how many decimal places to use.

Example

When considering the exam performance of boys and girls, it is reasonable to round both to 35%.

    If the data related to the school's exam performance in two consecutive years, and the rate was being tracked over several years, rounding to a whole number might not be sufficiently sensitive. When change is being studied, it is usually necessary to work to one, or perhaps two, decimal places and state the results as 34.9% and 35.1%.

Benefits of Percentages

- They make it easy to compare numbers.
- They make it easy to quantify how much something has changed.
- They make it easy to understand the relative importance when there are several elements represented in a data set.
- They are widely understood which makes them useful for communicating findings.

Disadvantages of Percentages

- They may not be meaningful when there are only a small number of values in the data set.
- It is essential to be clear about what is being measured and use the right numerator and denominator.

Example

Suppose in three consecutive years the price of a dress was £2.60, £2.75 and £2.95.

The percentage price increase in Year 1 is $\frac{£2.75 - £2.60}{£2.60} \times 100\% = 5.8\%$

In Year 2 $\frac{£2.95 - £2.75}{£2.75} \times 100\% = 7.3\%$ which is the percentage price increase in Year 2

$\frac{£2.95 - £2.60}{£2.60} \times 100\% = 13.5\%$ which is the percentage price increase between Year 1 and Year 3

Averages

The average is a figure that is most representative of all the values in a set of data. There are different methods of determining this figure and they usually produce different results. Irrespective of the method used, better insight is available when there are plenty of values in the data set. If there are only a few values, it is possible to perform the calculations but the result may not reveal anything about the subject. In historical research, understanding what any answer means, in the context of the data being averaged and the research topic, is as important as calculating a figure.

Mean Average

The mean average is the most widely used and is what many people understand an average to be.

To calculate the mean average, total all the values in the data set and divide the answer by the number of values in the data set.

Example

The number of prisoners jailed at a Victorian Court House from January to June were:

$$8+3+24+7+5+4 = 51$$

The number of terms in the set is 6
The mean average is 51 / 6 = 8.5

As in this example, the mean average is often a term that is not found in the data set. It can be a fraction, even if all the individual terms are whole numbers. When this happens, it is necessary to consider whether the item being averaged can be split in this manner when using the information.

Example

The above calculation reveals that 8.5 prisoners were jailed. In reality prisoners only exist as whole persons. When presenting findings a researcher would have to use appropriate terminology to describe the position and not refer to half of an actual person being jailed.

   If the figures related to a fine imposed, or the length of a jail sentence, it would reasonable to refer to £8.50 or 8 ½ weeks.

The value of the mean average is in the questions it generates. There are plenty of lines of enquiry to pursue raised by the data about convicted prisoners.

Example

An obvious point is that 8.5 is higher than all but one of the terms in the data set. This should trigger a question about whether the data is correct. It would be sensible to check that no error has been made with 24 by going back to the source of the figure, or even confirming it with another source.

Understanding why there was such an extreme value in March is important and checking the newspaper reports should provide an answer. There may have been a serious incident that month that resulted in a large number of people being taken to court, or perhaps an additional policeman had been employed. Alternatively, the answer could lie in the practices of the age. In Victorian times, special courts, known as the Assizes, were held in many towns twice a year to deal with serious crimes. If the Assizes were held in March it could explain the higher number.

Whatever the reason (or reasons), this investigation would probably split into two elements, the high number in March and the more usual position. If it was established that twenty of the prisoners were convicted at the Assizes and four at the local court it would be reasonable to recalculate the mean average to cover the local court only. This would give an indication of the likely level of a petty offenders being convicted in any month.

Benefits of the Mean Average

- It is straightforward to calculate.
- It uses all the values in a data set, eradicates the effect of high and low values and produces a more typical one.
- When a large number of values are being studied it can be difficult to keep them all in mind. Using one representative number can be helpful in understanding and explaining findings.
- It is widely used in more advanced statistical calculations.

Disadvantages of the Mean Average

- It can produce a result that is not possible for the topic being investigated.
- If there is an extremely high or low value in the data set (sometimes termed an outlier) the result may give a false impression of the topic being investigated.

Median Average

The median average is the middle value in a set of data and splits it into two equal parts. When there are an odd number of values there is one unambiguous median average. When there is an even number, there are two adjacent values from which the median is calculated.

To calculate the median average, list the data either from lowest to highest (or highest to lowest).

When there is an odd number of values in the list, divide the number of terms by 2 and add 0.5 to the answer. This gives the position of the middle value. Count to this position in the list to find the median item.

When there is an even number of values in the list, divide the number of values by 2. Count to this position in the list. The median average is the mean average of this item and the one that follows it.

Example

The following are the weekly wages of 6 Victorian coal miners, expressed in shillings.

19, 21, 23, 24, 26, 70.

To find the middle point, divide the number of values, 6, by 2 = 3
The third value highest to lowest is 24. The next value is 23.
The third value lowest to highest is 23. The next value is 24.
The difference between 24 and 23 = 1
1 divided by 2 = 0.5
24 – 0.5 = 23.5
23 + 0.5 = 23.5
The median average is 23.5

The median average, like the mean, can be a number that is not found within the data set. It can also be a fraction, even though all the values are whole numbers.

The relevance of the median average to a researcher can be demonstrated by comparing it with the mean average, which is (19+21+23+24+26+70)/6 = 30.5

At this pit, the very high salary of the site manager produces a result where five of the six employees earn less than the mean average wage. The median gives a much more representative position and allows a researcher to draw more meaningful conclusions about the worker's probable spending power and standard of living.

Benefits of the Median Average

- By ignoring extremes and focussing on a middle point, the median average is useful for identifying a typical situation.
- It can produce a more realistic answer than the mean when the data contains an extreme value.

Disadvantages of the Median Average

- It can produce a result that is not possible for the topic being investigated.
- The more extreme values in the data set may be overlooked. In historical research, the less typical results may contain important information.

A data set can be split into other numbers of equal parts. Quartiles (four), deciles (ten) and percentiles (a hundred) can sometimes be used in advanced investigations.

Mode Average

The mode average is the number that occurs most often in a set of data. This means that it will always be a value that is in the set.

To calculate the mode average, group similar items together.

Example

The number of occupants in a row of Victorian worker's cottages are
2,8,4,3,2,4,6,4,2,3

There are two methods for finding the mode.

Either list the items from lowest to highest (or highest to lowest)
2,2,2,3,3,4,4,4,6,8

Or list each item as a group.
2, 2, 2
8
4,4,4
3,3
6

Counting each group reveals which item is repeated most often, in this case 2 and 4.

Sometimes, as in the above example, there is not one single mode average. Statisticians disagree about whether, in this situation, there is no mode average or whether there are two. For a historical investigation, treat the data set as one that has two mode averages and study both. It is likely that the data was influenced by more than one issue. Even when a data set does produce a single mode, it can be revealing to work out the second and perhaps third most frequent items, to check what are the similarities and differences between them.

Example

The number of people living in the worker's cottages should trigger some questions. The popular view of the living conditions of Victorian workers is of large families crammed into tiny dwellings. In this row, most homes were occupied by either 2 or 4 people and the next most frequent occupancy was 3. Although the cottage with 8 people may have been overcrowded and the one with 6 cramped, it does not appear that overcrowding was the norm. Why was occupancy of these cottages low? Was it typical for the time and place?

Benefits of the Mode Average

- It pinpoints the usual position. This enables a researcher not to place too much emphasis on atypical examples.
- When two modes are not adjacent, or the first and second most frequent values are well separated, the data may be affected by more than one factor. This knowledge can help to focus an investigation.
- The mode can be used to explore data that is not expressed in numbers. Grouping and counting all the items in a set of data may reveal information that is not readily apparent from reading a list.

Example

A horticultural researcher who was interested in fashions in plants discovered that the favourite flower of twelve Edwardian gardeners was

Tulip, rose, sweet pea, carnation, lily, rose, lily, sweet pea, tulip, rose, sweet pea, rose,

This can be grouped

Tulip	2
Rose	4
Carnation	1
Lily	2
Sweet pea	3

It is now obvious which are the most and least frequent items in the list.

Disadvantages of the Mode

- There are situations when it is unlikely to produce valuable insights, for example, if several categories have similar numbers and one happens to have an extra entry. If a sample is small it may be worth adding some more examples where possible. If this does not alter the position, pursuing this line of investigation may not be worthwhile.

Putting an Investigation into Practice

The following demonstrates how a few straightforward calculations on a data set, and some thought about the results, can identify relevant patterns, and indicate where further research would be appropriate.

Example

Suppose the outcome of 11 successful libel claims resulted in awards of damages of:

£0.01, £75, £100, £100, £100, £100, £125, £200, £200, £200, £1000.

The mean average is £200
(£0.01+£75+£100+£100+£100+£100+£125+£200+£200+£200+£1000) /11

The median average (6th number in series, from top and bottom) is £100
The mode average (4 instances) is £100.

Comments:

In this case the mean average does not provide good insight. It is twice as high as the median and mode averages and the same as the second highest value, £200. It has also been affected by an extremely high and an extremely low value. It would be misleading to contend that £200 was the typical amount of damages that a claimant could expect to receive in damages.

This median and the mode averages are each £100. As the median represents the middle value and the mode represents the most frequent, this suggests that the 6 cases where damages range from £75–£125 are likely to be typical and may have features in common.

The second most frequent award was £200, which was given in 3 cases. These cases could be checked for any similarities between them and also any ways in which they differed from those where the damages were £75–£125.

The lowest and the highest results can be seen to be outliers, just by looking at the data. Discovering why these two cases had the outcomes they did is a valuable exercise. It may simply be that the person was lucky or unlucky. However, courts sometimes awarded a very small amount of compensation for a claim that was correct in law, but offended the moral standards of the age. Similarly a jury might be very generous with damages if the claimant had suffered exceptional harm, or if the defendant had behaved very badly. Understanding non-typical results may reveal something about the individual case, or about wider social values.

The mode average, £100, which has 4 occurrences, could be expressed as a percentage of the data set of 11. This is 36.4%. The next most common outcome, £200, has 3 occurrences and makes up 27.3% of the data set. Although 11 is too small a sample to draw general conclusions from, if there are common features in the two groups and distinguishing ones between them, it may indicate points to be alert to in further research.

More Advanced Techniques

Averages and percentages will enable a researcher to begin to investigate or quantify their data. For some studies this level of analysis will be sufficient.

As confidence with handling and interpreting numbers grows, a researcher may wish to carry out other investigations.

Frequency

Working out how often several different outcomes occur, will provide much more information about a subject than looking at just the one or two most popular. It also enables results to be shown in a graphical or tabular format, which may help in presenting them to other people. Expressing each category also as a

Example

The following numbers represent the amount of money in £'s spent by ten customers on food and drink in a hostelry on a bank holiday during the 1920s.

1, 1, 1
2, 2
3
5, 5
7
8

This can be converted into a frequency chart or table

Amount	Number of Customers (frequency)	Percentage %
£1	3	30
£2	2	20
£3	1	10
£5	2	20
£7	1	10
£8	1	10
	10	100

Once the data is in this form, it should trigger questions. Were the customers who spent £5, £7 or £8 in a group and those who spent less sole travellers? Were the customers who spent the lower amounts too poor to afford anything else, or were they in a hurry, or did they have just drinks rather than food? What do the reasons indicate about the type of person who frequented the hostelry? Why did no-one spend £4 or £6? How did the trade on a bank holiday differ from that on days that were not holidays? How did the takings compare with those for the hostelry across the road? It may not be possible to pursue each line of enquiry but the answers to some may reveal new insights.

percentage enables the researcher to remain aware of the relative proportion of each frequency to the whole.

Finding the frequency means developing work that has been done to discover the mode average. When creating any frequency chart or table, it is sensible to total the frequency column as this will guard against missing something, or counting an item twice.

Sometimes there are a very large number of individual frequencies and it may be appropriate to group them in bands.

Example

The amount spent in the restaurant could be expressed as

Amount	Number of Customers (frequency)	Percentage %
£0.01–£2	5	50
£2.01- £4	1	10
£4.01- £6	2	20
£6.01- £8	2	20
	10	100

Moving Averages

Moving averages can be used when analysing the same piece of information that is collected at different times, such as the highest daily temperature or the closing price of a commodity on a stock exchange. Moving averages need enough items to demonstrate an unambiguous trend, so they are not useful with small data sets.

To calculate a moving average, decide what period to average. There are no rules about this, it is a matter of judgement in each case. Then add the first values together until that number is reached and calculate the mean average. Continue by repeating the process but beginning with the second, and then the third value until all the values have been used.

Example

The following numbers represent the number of pots per batch that were broken whist they were being fired in a Staffordshire kiln in 1902.

12, 9, 15, 6, 10, 23, 9, 11

For a three period moving average, calculate

(12+9+15)/3, (9+15+6)/3 (15+6+10)/3 (6+10+23)/3 (10+23+9)/3 (23+9+11)/3

The moving average is 12, 10, 10.33, 13, 14, 14.33

This has smoothed the potentially distorting effect of 6 and 23. It suggests that the number of damaged pots is increasing, though the data set is small. In practice more data would need to be studied in order to come to a good conclusion.

In a moving average, there are always fewer resultant values than original data. The initial and final values in the data set do not have an average to set against them. If one is required, find the comparable information for the periods immediately prior to or after the data set to establish the missing terms.

Benefits of Moving Averages

- They are useful when investigating change over a period of time because they help to smooth peaks and troughs in the data. This will enable the underlying position to be established.
- They can be helpful when analysing data that is subject to regular seasonal fluctuation.
- They are a useful way of presenting fluctuating data when a trend has been proven.

Disadvantages of Moving Averages

- They may mask extreme values. The reason for any extreme may be relevant to understanding the topic.
- They are not appropriate for small data sets.
- The moving average may not reveal anything significant.

Other Statistical Measures

There are many other statistical techniques available to a researcher but these are beyond the scope of this book. Using some of these techniques may be necessary if working with an incomplete data set or to determine degree of accuracy provided by a calculation. Statistics can be used to identify the number of items to include in a sample, whether the conclusions revealed by a study of a sample are representative of the whole population from which the sample was drawn, or that an identified difference is significant rather than caused by chance.

Conclusion

For the historian, numbers are a tool for understanding an aspect of the past, not an end in themselves. Not all analyses will yield meaningful results and being able to identify which data to investigate is more important than carrying out the calculations. Used perceptively, data analysis can offer insight, provide evidence, identify where more research would add depth and even reveal where no additional understanding would be gained.

Data analysis will enable a researcher to communicate the results of their investigation in an objective rather than a subjective manner. In studies where numbers are not presented, it is helpful to know that any assertions made in a piece of work can be backed up with appropriate evidence, if the conclusions are challenged.

Chapter 11

Data Handling using a Spreadsheet

C hapter 10 covered data analysis by manual methods to show the principles behind some common calculations. In practice, researchers do not have to carry out time-consuming manual procedures as computers can produce the answer almost instantaneously, using a spreadsheet. Spreadsheets were developed to simulate the worksheets that were used in accountancy and finance but they quickly began to be used for many other purposes. They are now generally packaged as part of the suite of tools in desktop office products, such as *Excel* with *Microsoft Office*, *Calc* with *LibreOffice* and *Numbers* with *Apple iWork* and are widely available forms of software.

A spreadsheet is a piece of software that stores information in rows and columns in a grid. The point where a row and a column intersect is known as a cell. Each cell is specified by a reference such as A2, M31, T45 or W108. The letter or letters refer to the column and move left to right across the spreadsheet in alphabetical order. The number refers to the row, counting from top to bottom. Cell references are important because they may need to be specified in a formula.

Spreadsheets are created by a user from a very basic template. This makes them a very flexible tool for a researcher. It is not necessary to be an IT expert or highly numerate to use a modern spreadsheet, as providers have now made a range of options available simply by clicking an icon on the screen.

As with all IT, the only way to gain the basic skills and confidence to use spreadsheets successfully is hands-on familiarity. Spend some time investigating what they can do. Some people approach this by entering data and mastering one function at a time, moving onto another as confidence develops. Others set themselves a definite task and work out how to perform it, whilst another group might opt to follow tutorial exercises from a book or attend lessons. Whichever method is preferred, the initial skills to develop are entering data, formatting cells, sorting entries into order based on different attributes and performing straightforward calculations. Many people who become confident with the basics find that their skills continue to grow and become more advanced than they might have envisaged.

Spreadsheets allow many tasks to be carried out by more than one method. It is only necessary to know one, so choose whatever seems the easiest, whether it is using a menu or clicking on an icon.

Learning how to use a spreadsheet needs to take place very early in the research and well before any deadline is looming. Quality insights are unlikely to follow if a user is struggling with the software, and understanding from the outset what a spreadsheet can do may assist with decisions about what to record and how. If data from the investigation is used in the learning process, make sure that there is another copy to revert to. Even experienced users can make mistakes and accidentally delete something or not be able to work out how to undo an action.

Benefits of Spreadsheets in Historical Research

- They are much quicker than manual methods for sorting, analysing and calculating.
- They are very flexible and allow a researcher to set up something bespoke for a project.
- They can store much more data than a researcher is likely to have to record.
- They store data very compactly in comparison with manual records.
- A mistake can be corrected without spoiling the appearance of the worksheet.
- They eliminate the rechecking that is necessary with manual processing.
- They can instantly perform calculations involving a large number of items.
- They allow data to be quickly sorted and analysed in a variety of ways.
- They allow variables within the data to be compared easily.
- Results can be produced as graphs which can help with interpretation and presentation.
- More fields and records can be added at any time so it is possible to extend an investigation.
- They can search on multiple fields which allows sub-sets of data to be investigated.

Drawbacks with Spreadsheets for Historical Research

Many of the drawbacks with spreadsheets would also be issues with a manual approach.

- It may not be easy to change the layout once the project is under way.
- Data can be entered inaccurately.
- If they are given an incorrect instruction they will produce the wrong result.
- It can be tempting to collect data for its own sake or perform unnecessary analyses.
- It may not be possible to see all of the information on the computer screen.
- Print outs can require several sheets, or be too small to read.
- It is possible to lose data, so good back-up routines are essential.

Developing a Spreadsheet to Analyse

Data cannot be analysed until it has been input, so the first task to work on is configuring the grid of rows and columns into something suitable. Normally a spreadsheet will be set up so that that each row represents an item in the study and each column records information about the individual attributes that are being investigated. These attributes are usually known as fields.

- Begin by deciding which attribute is being recorded in each column and on the top line of the spreadsheet give the columns an appropriate heading. Use bold type for the heading so that it stands out.
- Think about how wide each column needs to be and set them to the required size. Fields that are going to contain writing will need to be wider than those that contain figures or a code. Try to strike a balance between not having the fields cramped up together and not having too many fields flowing off the screen. The width of any column can be adjusted at any time without causing problems so it does not matter if the first attempt is not perfect.
- Text that is too long for its field can cause a problem. Decide whether this should roll onto another line (known as wrapping) or whether it should be shrunk so that it fits in the field. When text is wrapped it automatically increases the height of its row. Text that is greatly reduced in size may not be legible.

- Consider the format in each column. The spreadsheet should have an option for setting a date format, a number format and a currency format so that all items in the column are automatically displayed in this way. When using numbers, decide how many decimal places are needed and select this. When using currency select £0.00 rather that £0, as any calculations performed on this data could end in pence even if all the data is in £s.
- Consider the alignment of data in each column. It is conventional for writing to be aligned to the left and numbers to the right. Centre alignment can sometimes be useful because it helps to give visual separation between fields.
- Make sure that the font is clear and easy to read. Fonts without embellishments are often the best ones to use.

Entering Data into a Spreadsheet

This is a straightforward process. Highlight the cell where the data is to be entered, move the cursor to the input line at the top of the spreadsheet and type in the data. Then press the *enter* key. The data will appear in the specified cell.

A quicker method is to highlight the cell where the data is to be entered and type it in. Then press the enter key.

Spreadsheets often try to predict the next word as it is being typed. If a word has already been used, the spreadsheet may offer it based on the first couple of letters. If it is correct, press the *enter* key and the whole entry will appear. Prediction is a useful feature if the same word is being repeated, such as the month, as it reduces repetitive typing. If the word being offered is wrong ignore it and keep typing. It will disappear as soon as the software realises that what is being entered does not match its suggestion.

When entering data do not use any cosmetic effects to make the spreadsheet look pleasing. There are times when it is helpful to make an entry stand out for a purpose connected with the research by making it bold, underlined, italic or a different colour. It is not sensible to have information that has been highlighted for research purposes fighting with special effects.

Analysing a Spreadsheet

When all the data has been entered, ensure that there are no empty fields and that the content of each cell seems reasonable. It is easy to key in a double figure or to miss a digit out and a visual check should highlight this. When the data has been reviewed and amended, if necessary, save the spreadsheet twice, using different names. Keep one file as a back up in case a problem occurs and do not use it for any other purpose. All analysis should be carried out using the other file. It is never worth the risk of not having a back up of data that is being analysed. If more than one analysis is being performed, it may be appropriate to take a back up after each.

The data on a spreadsheet is analysed by giving instructions to perform a process using the data in one or more cells and perhaps to display the result in another cell of the user's choice. As there are plenty of tools on a spreadsheet there is often more than one way of arriving at the same answer. Some users are very confident about constructing complex formulas or using templates, known as wizards, to get to the result in one step. Others are not. Not being ultra-confident with advanced features is no reason to avoid using a spreadsheet. The objective of a historical investigation is to answer a question about the past, not to use a sophisticated method to produce figures. Perform a calculation in several steps if necessary. It is better than making a mistake in setting up the formula and will still be much faster than using a manual method.

Arithmetic Functions

Any formula that is used in a historical investigation will probably use one or more of the four arithmetic functions. These are addition, (+) subtraction, (−) multiplication (*) and division (/).

In an arithmetic formula, one action may need to be performed before another. In this case the first action should be placed in brackets ( ).

Constructing a Formula

A user who understands the four arithmetical processes should be able to construct the formulas needed to perform calculations. It is just a matter of thinking logically and applying the process that would be used in a manual calculation. It does not matter whether letters are entered in upper or lower case.

Example

A4 =A1+A2+A3 means add the contents of Cell A1, Cell A2 and Cell A3 and display the answer in Cell A4

A4=A1:A3 means add the contents of Cell A1, Cell A2 and Cell A3 and display the answer in Cell A4

C5=A5-B5 means subtract the contents of Cell B5 from Cell A5 and display the answer in Cell C5

D6 = D5*3 means multiply the contents of Cell D5 by 3 and display the answer in Cell D6

E8 = A4/B7 means divide the contents of Cell A4 by the contents of Cell B7 and display the answer in Cell E8

When calculations are being performed, specify the format that is needed in the answer cell. Answers may be displayed to many decimal points unless the spreadsheet has been told to round the answer to the nearest whole number, or restrict it to the first one or two decimal places.

If the symbol ###### appears as the result of a calculation it usually means that the cell is too small to display the answer. Widen the column and the answer should appear.

Sometimes, an error message appears instead of an answer. This usually means that the specified calculation is impossible to perform. When this happens the spreadsheet often highlights what has been entered which is very helpful for spotting the error and correcting the formula.

Summation

Spreadsheets sometimes try to help a user by anticipating what they are trying to calculate. The Greek letter Σ (sigma) is used in statistics to mean the sum of. If there are a number of cells to be added, placing the cursor in the box where the answer is required and then clicking the Σ icon at the top of the spreadsheet will produce the answer without the need to enter a formula. This is helpful, but not foolproof. If there is data running vertically and horizontally the spreadsheet will have to guess which total is needed and may opt for the wrong one.

When using the Σ function, check that the right range of figures has been used. The spreadsheet normally highlights the cells making it easy to see. If it has picked up the wrong range, change the formula that will be displayed in the input box.

Calculating the Mean Average

Place the cursor in an empty cell, enter the = sign followed the cell references of the items to be totalled in brackets. Count the number of items to be totalled and divide by that number.

Example

=(B2+B3+B4+B5+B6+B7+B8+B9+B10)/9
or =(B2:B10)/9

Calculations often start at Row 2 because Row 1 is used for column headings.

Finding the Median Average

Use the sort into ascending (or descending) order icon at the top of the spreadsheet to put the data being averaged into order. The sort icon is usually an arrow pointing either up or down.

When data is being sorted it is important to keep everything about an item together. The spreadsheet will normally ask whether to sort just the highlighted column or all columns before it carries out the instruction.

When the data is in order, determine the middle point and count to this. If there is an even number of values, it will be necessary to find the mean average of the two central ones unless they are the same number.

Finding the Mode Average and Frequency Information

Using the sort that has been performed for the median average, count how many times each value occurs. The value that occurs most often is the mode average. It is usually possible to spot which are the largest categories so it may not be necessary to count every one, unless frequency is also being ascertained.

Recording Results

There are plenty of ways to record results, either on the spreadsheet itself or somewhere separate. It is surprising how quickly detail is forgotten, so never list results without adequate explanation such as total, mean average, or percentage of successful claims. This simple task will save time later trying to remember what a figure means and how it was calculated.

Graphs

The graph or chart function on a spreadsheet is worth mastering at an early stage. From the perspective of an investigation it is a useful tool for understanding some relationships between data. It is also a simple way of presenting findings. The graphs that are produced by the spreadsheet can be printed out or exported into other documents, which can save the researcher time and effort. Always remember when creating a graph that the important aspect is the information it conveys, not fancy effects or gimmicks which can be distracting.

Column

A column chart shows information in a vertical columnar format. It can be a way of ascertaining the mode average as this can be read off the vertical axis if the chart represents a frequency.

In addition to presentation, column charts can be very useful for studying the properties of a sample because it is sometimes possible to see whether the sample, and therefore its mean and median averages, are being affected by an extreme value. If the frequency has an obvious central peak, the data being investigated is balanced. If the peak is towards one edge it is being affected at one extreme. When using advanced statistical techniques it is necessary to know whether data is balanced or skewed.

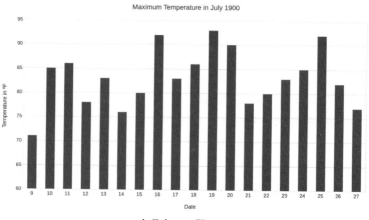

A Column Chart.

Bar

A bar chart shows the same information as a column chart but horizontally rather than vertically.

Line

Line charts represent information by a continuous line rather than in blocks. They are particularly useful when presenting data over a period of time.

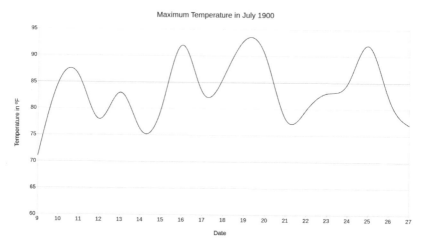

A Line Chart.

Pie

A pie chart shows frequency information as percentages of a circle. It is a very simple method of showing proportions and is a method of presentation that is readily understood by most people. It can be very helpful for conveying frequency information to people who are not confident about interpreting tables, or for presenting some headline points succinctly.

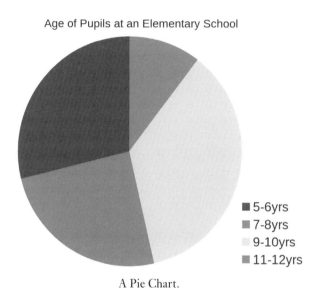

A Pie Chart.

Pie charts have limitations. It is not possible to read any figures from them. Nor are they very useful with a large number of items of very low frequencies because it is hard for the eye to see what is happening. If there are a number of these items it is usually worth combining them as 'other' for the purposes of clear presentation.

Scatter Charts

Scatter diagrams show the relationship between two sets of data, through a number of dots. If the dots are scattered randomly there is no relationship between the two items, but if they tend to form a line then a link is likely to exist. This is known as correlation. The points do not have to be in a perfectly straight line for a relationship between them to be identified.

Example

Extending the frequency example on page 102 about the money spent by ten customers in a hostelry, the number of people in each customer's party was inferred from the number of items on each bill.

Amount	Number in Party
£1	1
£1	2
£1	1
£2	2
£2	3
£3	4
£5	5
£5	6
£7	6
£8	7

This can be represented on a scatter chart as follows

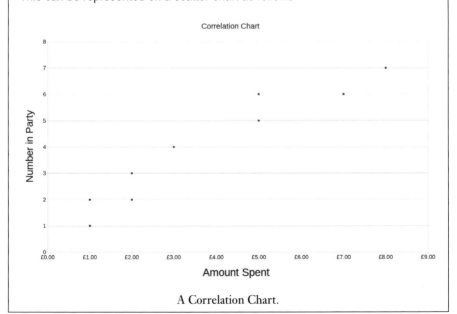

A Correlation Chart.

The points are not in a perfectly straight line, but it is clear there is a strong link between the amount spent and the number of people in each group.

As the link between number in party and size of bill is strong, there would be little to be gained from trying to answer one of the initial questions about the data sample, why no-one spent £4 or £6.

Sometimes correlation arises not from the two sets of data being tested but from some other factor that links them.

Example

A seaside music hall notices that when its matinee performance is sold out, its café sells many cups of tea but very few glasses of lemonade. Direct correlation exists between sales of tickets and hot drinks because both go up at the same time. Inverse correlation exists between between sales of tickets and cold drinks because as one rises the other falls.

Both relationships are caused by a factor that is not being studied, the weather. On a cool, wet day holidaymakers tend to visit the theatre and drink warm beverages. On a warm one they enjoy the sunshine rather than sitting indoors.

Scatter charts must always be interpreted with intelligence because there are situations when correlation exists between two variables but there is no causal link that can be found to explain it.

Example

Correlation between men with the forename Henry and a guilty verdict at the Assize Court would not indicate that men named Henry are likely to have criminal tendencies.

Correlation between men with the surname Henry and a guilty verdict at the Assize Court may indicate that there was a criminal family in the area.

Scatter diagrams are an extremely versatile tool for historical investigation as they enable a dataset with several variables to be tested pair by pair. The results should highlight relationships where further research may prove beneficial and the lines of investigation that are not worth pursuing. Once correlation between two variables has been established, this is only relevant if the researcher can explain what it means in the context of the subject being studied. Correlation is a tool, it is not an answer or a reason. Far from being the outcome of an investigation, finding a link between two variables may be just the beginning.

After an Investigation

It is perfectly acceptable to extend a study by adding more items into a spreadsheet after it has been analysed but always keep a separate copy of the data that was studied. Someone may challenge the findings or they may need to be reviewed in light of further work. If it is not possible to identify the exact information that was used, conclusions may lack credibility and the researcher may find it difficult to understand any differences between the original sample and the expanded one. Keeping a copy of important data on a memory stick prevents data loss if the computer develops a fault.

If expanding an investigation involves inserting more columns or rows into a worksheet after it has been analysed, check that a formula is properly specifying what is needed before relying on any updated answer. Often a formula adjusts automatically to take account of changes but this cannot be guaranteed.

Advanced Statistical Techniques

Modern spreadsheets have routines that guide users to calculate statistical measures. They also have an extensive help function. This guides users to a method for practically any analysis they may wish to perform, so it is not necessary to remember every formula. Carrying out any calculation is far less relevant than being able to select appropriate investigations and interpret the results. There is no merit in obtaining a wealth of statistical information if it does not give any additional insight into the topic, or if the researcher is unable to to see what that insight is.

Conclusion

It is not necessary to be an IT expert to use a spreadsheet in a historical investigation. Confidence with just a few simple techniques can reduce the time needed to calculate and then recheck answers. This means that there is more time to understand and interpret the results.

Spreadsheets can store large amounts of data and process it quickly, which makes it feasible for a researcher to work with a larger sample than when manual methods are being used, or to compare more variables. This can quickly highlight the areas where new insights into the subject might be discovered and help to avoid pursuing ideas that are unlikely to lead to a better understanding of the past. It might also enable a researcher to include sufficient items to make the results of a study generalisable to the total population.

Chapter 12

Using Spreadsheets in a Historical Study

S preadsheets can be used to record data as an alternative to a database. They cannot replace specialist databases such as *Gramps* which are used by family historians who are discovering their family tree. If the researcher needs a good view of their data, or if the study will involve statistical analyses, a spreadsheet may be the best choice.

Spreadsheets can be a useful tool for historical investigations even if the study does not involve numerical data. Items in a spreadsheet can be sorted alphabetically making it possible to look for patterns and relationships in names, occupations, places of residence or any other factor. If a piece of data is factual it may be feasible to record it by name. If it is expressing a situation it may be necessary to devise and use a code.

A spreadsheet is a very flexible method for data recording because it can be designed to capture whatever information is needed. It is wise to make full use of its capabilities by splitting information into plenty of categories and recording each aspect in its own column. This aids analysis and makes it easy to see if something has not been recorded.

When setting up a spreadsheet from newspaper sources, three fields should always be included: source, date and additional information.

Source

This is important as it authenticates the rest of the record and enables it to be located easily. Usually the name of the newspaper and date of publication are sufficient. To prevent this taking up too much screen space, the cell storing source information can be kept small and the text size reduced as it is rarely needs to be read. If necessary, the information can easily be viewed by highlighting the cell, which makes the entry appear full size in the input box.

Date

The date should include at least the year and the month. Date information makes it possible to sort entries into chronological order, and focus on a shorter period within the data set if necessary. The date is crucial for identifying when there may be gaps or imbalance in a sample that covers a period of time. It also makes it possible to study how something develops over the years. When working with a spreadsheet it is helpful to store items so that they appear chronologically on screen, so sort them into order at the end of an input session, or use the insert row option to get them into the right order whilst inputting.

Additional Information

It is inevitable that there will be unusual features about some items that need to be recorded. This could be as varied as an assumption about the data, a note that a report offers good insight into a topic, that the case might be a good one to include as an example, or perhaps further investigation of it is required. Storing this as additional information keeps the research in one place rather than becoming scattered in other notes. If the same point is regularly being included as Additional Information, decide whether it should be incorporated as a separate field as soon as this becomes apparent.

Devising the Spreadsheet

At the start of an investigation it may not be obvious which will be the most productive aspects and it is worth taking a little time to read through a few newspaper reports before creating a spreadsheet. As the concerns of the past are not necessarily the concerns of the present, it may become apparent that certain information needed for a study was not recorded, or perhaps an unexpected angle could present itself. Although it is possible to insert extra fields at any point, backtracking to collect detail whose significance was not initially appreciated can waste time. Bear in mind that, unless the number of items in the study is small, it will not be feasible to check every one before settling on the data to be collected. At some stage, usually early on in the study, reasoned decisions about what to record will have to be taken.

When a field on a spreadsheet is sorted, items will be listed in numerical or alphabetical order. Thinking carefully about this aspect when designing a spreadsheet can avoid problems when analysing it.

Name

A 'name' identifies an item and needs a field of its own. It can be the name of a person, a company or perhaps the plaintiff and defendant in a court case. When using the name of a person, it is better to use surname followed by first name rather than vice versa. Data in surname order may be relevant but an alphabetical list of forenames is not likely to be needed. If data might need to be sorted by forename and surname, use two columns.

Address

If the address of any premises is included, consider how to deal with the number. A study is more likely to want to analyse a whole road rather than all premises whose number is twelve. Using one field for the premises number (or name) and the next field for other address details would allow the data to be grouped by road or number.

Age

Old newspapers did not routinely report a person's age and when they did, the report sometimes included an opinion based on the individual's appearance rather than an accurate figure. Even at the beginning of the twentieth century older people could be very hazy about their age. There are also instances of an individual being described as a few years older or younger than someone else.

As it can be difficult to establish a person's age beyond reasonable doubt, always decide how accurate this information needs to be. In many cases it will be possible to use an age band such as 51-60 in the study. This eliminates any difficulties with a person who is described as 'about 55' and a sister who is 'a couple of years younger'.

It is sensible to record any 'best estimate' data in a different style on the spreadsheet such as in italics, underlined, or in a coloured font so that it can be spotted easily and taken into account when interpreting any results if this seems necessary. Best estimate data will not be acceptable if absolute precision is required.

Occupation

A person's occupation is a very useful piece of information. Not only does it show how the person was earning their living, it can be used as a proxy for other data, such as a person's likely social class and position, how they may have been regarded by others, values they may have held and their financial standing and spending power.

Occupation can be a challenging category to record and analyse because there were so many trades, crafts and professions a person could earn their living from and a number of levels at which they could be working. Unless fine detail is necessary, standardise terms as much as possible. A maid, housemaid, parlourmaid, lady's maid, scullery maid, kitchen maid and cook could all be described as servants, as could a butler, footman, coachman, valet and gentleman's gentleman.

The generic term shopkeeper can be used to describe a butcher, draper, grocer, greengrocer, ironmonger and tobacconist whilst craftsman might reasonably include plumbers, carpenters, cordwainers and smiths.

Sometimes, however, the breadth of an occupation can be so wide it can be almost meaningless. A farmer, for example, was someone who made a living from the land, irrespective of whether he owned thousands of fertile acres and employed an army of men to cultivate them, or rented a tiny holding from which he scraped a living. When dealing with farmers, it is always worth using *FarmerL*, *FarmerM* and *FarmerS* to distinguish between the large, moderate and small. It may also be useful to record whether someone is self-employed or an employee, perhaps by a term such as *CraftsmanS* or *CraftsmanE*.

Women, and young unmarried men, may have been described with reference to the head of household's occupation, rather than their own, (if they had one). When recording occupation, decide which is more relevant to the research if the head of household's is also given. The unmarried daughter of a self-employed man may have worked in the same type of occupation as the daughter of one of her father's employees, but would they have shared the same values or spending power?

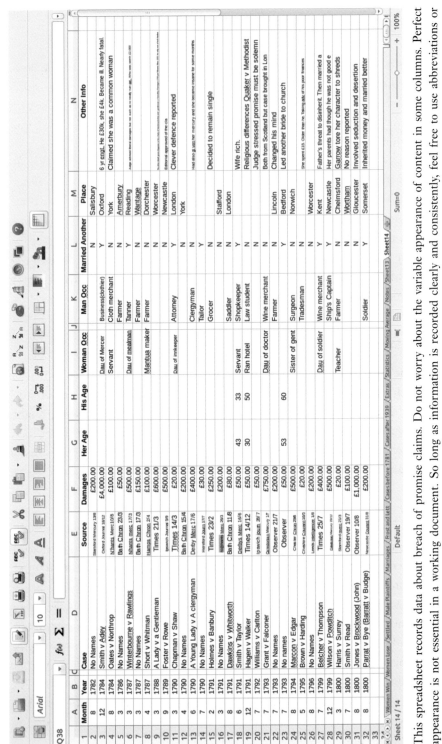

This spreadsheet records data about breach of promise claims. Do not worry about the variable appearance of content in some columns. Perfect appearance is not essential in a working document. So long as information is recorded clearly and consistently, feel free to use abbreviations or customise columns in different ways. Note also the icons across the top of the spreadsheet which are used for customising the spreadsheet and also for carrying out some types of analysis. Tabs at the bottom allow a variety of different sheets to be created.

It can be helpful to use two adjacent columns to record occupation data. Listing a person's actual job preserves variety and can reveal how the economy or social structure functioned. Listing a simplified version, or even devising and entering a code, makes analysis much more straightforward and can prevent general themes and patterns becoming lost in a welter of detail.

Place

This is another useful category as it can pinpoint differences between regions or between the urban and the rural. A point to remember is that a village, town or county may have changed its name or boundaries over the years. This can be relevant when carrying out comparisons over time. Place is important in identifying any gaps or imbalance in a sample that purports to cover the whole country.

Financial Data

The value of money alters unpredictably with time and there can be step changes also, such as in 1971 when Britain changed its currency. If any pre-decimal financial data is included, it is advisable to convert to the decimal equivalent, as spreadsheets cannot perform calculations on the old format. Details of how to convert currency are included in Appendix 4. A similar point applies to old weights and measures.

How Many Aspects Should be Investigated?

This can only be answered on a case by case basis, as it depends on what the researcher hopes to discover about their subject. General studies, or studies that span a long time period, may need to consider more elements than one which sets out to investigate a specific question or a short time frame. Researchers who do not wish to study a large number of variables, or whose time is limited, may decide to restrict the number of aspects they have to deal with by keeping their project specific. A useful approach is to devise a project which could be progressively developed so that it builds up into something much bigger. The findings of a study that was limited to a single town or year can be tested by repeating the investigation for other localities or looking at the same town a few years earlier or later.

As a substantial amount of time and effort can be spent locating and reading newspaper reports, it makes sense to capture any important facts that are mentioned regularly, even if the need for them is not readily apparent. There would probably have been a good reason at the time for the identical fact being reported so often. Be discriminating about peripheral detail. A woman's age might correlate with other features and provide valuable learning. It is unlikely that the colour of her hair would be relevant to many topics.

If an element of the subject has already been studied widely and there is consensus about it, collecting another set of detailed data may be a poor use of time, unless the researcher wishes to challenge previous findings or to use the information in a different manner.

When studies cover a wide time period, be prepared for the amount and type of information to alter. The issue being investigated could have been affected by an external factor, such as a change in the law. Social attitudes are also relevant and if a topic became more fashionable or less interesting to newspaper readers, the frequency and content of reports may have altered to reflect this.

Data Completeness

At an early stage, a researcher will have to decide what information is needed before an item can be included in a study. While it is tempting to think 'everything', in reality this is unlikely to be achieved because some newspaper reports were less detailed than others. Being too rigid about data completeness could render a study impossible because there are insufficient cases in the sample. There are statistical techniques which can determine the degree of inaccuracy arising from missing data and it may be possible to draw reasonable conclusions from data sets that have a few items missing. This is another reason for using more than the bare minimum of cases when conducting a historical study, as it helps to address the issues that arise when data is incomplete.

Do not reject any item before the analysis stage of an investigation. It is possible that the missing data was included in another newspaper. Always keep a note of any item rejected because of insufficient data. Incomplete items are part of the total number and the fact that newspapers did not think certain detail worth recording may suggest something about attitudes of the time.

Locating missing data

It is unusual for a single newspaper report to contain every piece of data needed in a study. When a historian has finalised a sample and extracted the information required, it is likely that some gaps or discrepancies will remain, even if more than one newspaper has been checked. At this point, the researcher has to decide whether to chase detail that might never have been recorded or proceed without it. Always ensure that the most relevant newspapers have been consulted before accepting that data is not available.

• If the initial source was a national newspaper, a local one may have further information.
• The most likely newspaper to carry a detailed account is one that is local to the event in question.
• A well-structured query on the search page of a provider that has several newspapers might identify one that contains the missing details.

There are occasions when trying to fill in gaps is not a good use of time.

• If the same piece of data is missing from many entries it may never have been recorded.
• If it is already clear that no useful learning will result from that aspect of the investigation.
• If resolving a minor discrepancy will not improve the analysis in any way.

Inference

Some pieces of data can be found by inference. If the weekly wage is known, annual earnings can be worked out. If the weekly rent is known, it may be feasible to form a view about the type of housing a person lived in, based on knowledge of the period and place in question.

The dividing line between inference and guesswork can be a fine one. It is always better to leave a gap than to guess, as the latter will lead to false conclusions. Gaps do not reflect badly on a conscientious researcher who has made sufficient effort to find a piece of data and concluded that it is not available.

Reasonableness of Data

When as much data as possible has been located, review it for reasonableness before analysing it. Take care with numbers because they cannot be relied on to scan well. If any number seems out of line, check the information, preferably with a different newspaper.

Analysis Involving Incomplete Data

If a large number of items are being investigated, valid learning can arise when there are gaps in data, so long as there are not too many of them. If there is only a small number of items, forming conclusions is more problematic. Any investigation that involves incomplete data must have regard for what is missing and only draw conclusions that can be substantiated.

Example

If a group of 20 prisoners was made up of 9 men, 5 women and 6 whose gender is unknown, it would be valid to state that it comprised between 45 per cent and 75 per cent men depending on the unknown data. It would also be valid to state that it comprised between 25 per cent and 55 per cent women depending on the unknown data. This is a very wide range and it is frustrating not to be able to get more accuracy.

Trying to achieve this by assigning a gender to the unknowns in some arbitrary fashion would be misleading, as would ignoring the 6 unknowns and calculating figures based on a sample size of 14.

If the group comprised 200 people and the gender of 6 was not known, it would be possible to form valid conclusions based on the 194 pieces of data that were known.

Good historical investigations take the evidence that is available and respect it. Even when it only provides a low level of insight, it may be an advance on the previous position. Trying to obtain better accuracy by adjusting for unknowns, without having a valid basis for doing so, is the hallmark of a mediocre historian. Attempting to take advantage of gaps in evidence to construct results that 'prove' an outcome desired by the researcher is the sign of an unethical approach.

Interpreting Results

Although computers are excellent at crunching numbers, the answers they generate are not an end in themselves, and are rarely informative without further work by a researcher to interpret them.

Newspapers themselves are a good place to start as they might contain editorials or readers' letters that put some or all of the findings into context. If editorials and letters appear to contradict the research findings, consider why. It may be that people at that time had a wrong perception of an issue, perhaps because they did not have the more unbiased information that a researcher is now able to locate and study.

Good research inevitably leads to further questions, so do not settle for one set of analyses. Be prepared to select subsets of the data and investigate them further. If 75 per cent of cases have very similar features, consider performing two separate investigations rather than blurring distinctions with averages.

Analyses that cover many years may be insensitive to any legal, social and economic changes that were affecting the issue. It may be necessary to look at the data on a decade by decade basis, use a moving average or adjust all monetary values for inflation in order to obtain good insight.

Presenting Results

When presenting results, always disclose any assumptions that have been made and any gaps or other limitations in the data. It is better to be open on this point from the outset, rather than risk someone else undermining the research by pointing out flaws. It is not always possible to obtain a perfect set of data and it does not denote poor research, so long as appropriate effort has been made to obtain the information.

If findings are illustrated by case studies, the most interesting examples, or the ones where most information is available in newspapers, may be atypical. These should not be ignored if they reveal something about the issue or society of the time, but the study should also include some examples that are typical. If a study of legal cases showed that the most frequent sum given as damages was £50 and it was usually to a young married man, including one case that contained these elements would be appropriate, even if it was not intrinsically interesting.

	A	B	C	D	E	F	G	H	I	J
		Chapter		Words Plan	Words Actual		Status		Learning Outcomes	
1										
2										
3		Contents		100	125	80%	Needs checking against text			
4		Introduction		500	425	90%				
5										
6		1 History of Newspapers		4,000	4,250	100%				
7		Development of newspaper industry							Understanding how the GB press developed, key titles and the differences between publications	
8		Key titles								
9		Taxes and government attitudes								
10		Increasing literacy								
11		Changes in printing and distribution technology								
12		Daily and weekly								
13		Local, regional, national								
14										
15										
16		2 The News Chain		2,000	2,775	95%	Final review needed			
17		How news was collected, reported and sold							Understanding the process and role of different people and the implications for what was in a newspaper	
18		Journalists, editors, proprietors								
19		Non-technical staff								
20										
21		3 Content of a Newspaper		3,500	3,850	95%	Final review needed			
22		Editorial							Understanding the different types of material available and what each section of a newspaper might reveal about the past	
23		News								
24		Parliamentary and legal reports								
25		Opinion features								
26		Readers letters								
27		Specialist advice columns								
28		Births, marriages and death notices								
29		Stories and puzzles								
30		Pictures and Cartoons					Detailed discussion moved to a separate chapter			
31		Advertisements								
32										
33										

This is part of a spreadsheet used solely by the author to plan and to monitor progress when writing this book. Column F, which represents how complete the author considered each chapter, was left unheaded to save screen space. When a spreadsheet is to be shared, ensure that everything is clear and always use headings. Also consider the positioning of columns. As the percentage is not calculated from the numbers that precede it, perhaps the layout should be changed to avoid inadvertent confusion?

Further Uses of Spreadsheets

This chapter has concentrated on using a spreadsheet to collect and analyse data. Spreadsheets can be used for many other purposes, such as planning research, recording what has been done, or analysing some items in further detail.

Modern spreadsheets have a row of tabs at the bottom which open further sheets. Always make full use of this facility. It is an excellent way of keeping all aspects of a piece of research together and makes switching between the different records very easy.

Conclusion

The purpose of this chapter is to give ideas about how to make use of the database technique with spreadsheets, rather than being a prescriptive way of how to collect data. Each individual researcher must decide what data to collect and how to record it.

For anyone who would like to consolidate this introduction to historical investigations covered in Chapters 9-12, a worked example is included at the end of the main text. Anyone who would like to understand the full range of statistical techniques that are available to a researcher should consult a suitable text book.

Chapter 13

Illustrations in Newspapers

Illustrations became staple content in many newspapers, magazines and periodicals in the nineteenth and early-twentieth centuries. To their first viewers, they revealed an exotic, exciting, perhaps frightening world that lay beyond their experience of local town or village life. To the modern researcher, who has grown up seeing the world through visual media and perhaps travelled to some of its far-flung outposts, old illustrations still reveal an exciting world, but one that has now largely disappeared.

The earliest drawings survive in periodicals and magazines from the eighteenth century. Along with portraits of famous people, a number of exquisite and high quality images of architecture and nature show what the presses of the age were capable of reproducing. At that time, picture printing was a complex and time-consuming process that was not viable for products with a short life. Illustrations were rare in the newspapers of the period and were usually restricted to an embellished initial letter of an article, or to a motif or logo placed above some text. Occasionally, more complex printing was considered worthwhile because some newspapers included a few tables, charts and maps.

By the early-nineteenth century, a sketched logo might be featured in an advertisement, together with written information about the business or the product it was selling. Some compositors had begun to consider presentation because, on occasions, the logo or motif that topped an article indicated its content, such as a horse heading a piece about the races. These illustrations were simple. A few rare exceptions related to events of extraordinary national importance. *The Times* first included a picture when it depicted the funeral carriage of Lord Nelson in 1806 and it subsequently illustrated a few other royal events with sketches of increasing complexity. More than thirty years later, drawings of Queen Victoria's coronation were published by several papers.

By the time of the coronation, change was in the air and images were beginning to appear on the front page of some publications. Noticing that pictures usually secured better sales, newsagent Herbert Ingram conceived the idea for a new

Drawings of foreign lands such as the Matterhorn in Switzerland revealed a new world to their nineteenth century audience. (*Author's Collection*)

weekly newspaper which launched in May 1842 as *The Illustrated London News*. Thirty-two woodcut prints, scattered throughout the paper, accompanied news stories from Britain and around the world. It was a triumphant first and, within a decade, several more illustrated newspapers were serving a voracious market. These sprang up alongside established newspapers, which did not rush to be at the forefront of this innovation.

The visual revolution of the 1840s was stimulated by improved technology. Rather than having to print pictures and words in two separate processes, a method of compositing was devised which enabled etched drawings and written material to be placed side by side in the master printing block. The speed at which any newspaper could acquire the new technology was one factor determining whether it included illustrations or not. Another was the increased production cost that the newspaper would incur by employing artists, especially if it published daily. Class may also have been a factor, with pictures regarded as a sign of someone whose reading skills were less honed and whose tastes were perhaps less refined. Readers of the established newspapers seemed content to receive the news in words alone. Whether they also purchased one or more of the illustrated papers was another matter.

Nineteenth Century Drawings

From the 1840s, until the end of the century, newspaper illustrations were of a high technical standard. They consisted of detailed drawings that were etched onto wood or metal and printed in black and white. Many drawings were accurate representations of their subject, because illustrators worked from detailed sketches made by artists who were on-site when a news story broke and who captured the immediate detail. As photography became more reliable, engravers were able to work from photographs as well as sketches.

The illustrations in the weekly publications covered a wide range of subjects and gave the reader the experience and emotions of being an eyewitness to major events. They included being present at the aftermath of a coal mining disaster, attending the opening of a new engineering marvel, observing a prestigious royal occasion, surveying the battlefield where a war was being fought on foreign soil or visiting an exhibition to see the latest work of a renowned artist. Well over a century later, these illustrations retain the power to bring aspects of the past to life.

In contrast to the authentic situations presented by *The Illustrated London News*, a different form of visual journalism was pioneered by *The Illustrated Police News* from 1864. Now regarded as the first tabloid newspaper, it hooked its buyers with imaginative representations of the bizarre and sensational events of the previous week emblazoned across the front page and the promise of more inside. Scandalous court cases, tragic accidents and melodramatic crimes were all portrayed with consummate technical skill and a degree of artistic licence, as it seems improbable that some of the scenes would have been observed by a passing artist or photographer.

The daily newspapers took longer to incorporate illustrations and when they did, the first pictures were generally simple, straightforward sketches, compared with the elaborate artistic images that graced the weeklies. Notable in these early illustrations is a restrained attitude towards people who were in the news. It was unusual for anyone whose character was perceived as good to have their likeness made public, unless they were a public figure. Finding a picture or sketch of an ordinary person in the papers of the nineteenth century often suggests that, in the newspaper's eyes, the individual had somehow offended against society.

Twentieth Century Photographs

Photographs began to be used more widely in the early twentieth century and newspapers gradually combined words and images when presenting stories. Photography only became feasible for newspapers when cameras were able to take good quality pictures that retained enough detail after printing on the low quality paper used by newspapers. It was also necessary to design and manufacture the equipment necessary for photographs to be reproduced directly. When technology had progressed to this point, it was cheaper, and less labour intensive, to print photographs than to employ artists and engravers. It may also have brought a greater degree of veracity to the news-giving process in the eyes of some readers. An artist could emphasise or omit something, but the camera did not lie.

The balance of content in newspapers between words and illustrations changed around the start of the twentieth century. The main reason was the emergence of a market for news amongst the newly literate working class, many of whom did not have the advanced reading skills needed to cope with columns of dense printing in the existing publications.

Even when photography was an established medium, newspapers did not necessarily include pictures of people in the news. Camera film was slow and lenses were bulky, making it difficult to capture reluctant subjects from a distance. Editors also may have been reticent about upsetting someone influential in a society still defined by wealth, status and privilege.

As the twentieth century progressed, a visual element became essential to many stories and, in some situations, the picture was the most important feature, telling a story in a way that words could not. Pictures of people from all walks of life, and in a variety of situations, became commonplace and most newspapers tried to include an image of anyone who was involved in an important story. People in some occupations began to exploit the potential for newspaper coverage that showed them as attractive individuals. Newspapers differed in how they adapted to this. Some concentrated on visual content, while others prioritised the quality of writing and the depth of analysis. The marketplace was wide and readers could opt for the approach they preferred.

Cartoons

Newspapers developed from the very diverse printing industry of the seventeenth century, with a mainly respectable content, as editors fearful of a sojourn in jail, tried to stay within the law.

Flourishing alongside them in those early years was a more disreputable, visual type of journalism, represented by pamphlets, prints and broadsheets which poked fun at the establishment and risked the wrath of the law tumbling onto the heads of those who wrote, drew or printed them. Unsurprisingly these publications were often anonymous. This disrespectful, scurrilous branch of journalism eventually provided respectable newspapers with one of their most identifiable forms of visual content: the cartoon.

The original meaning of the word cartoon is a preparatory sketch by an artist, capturing in a few pen strokes the essentials of an idea that will be developed in a work of art. Newspaper cartoons, which depicted their subject in strong outlines, purloined their name from the artistic technique they resembled. *Punch* magazine, which included cartoons from its inception in the 1840s, has been credited with appropriating the term.

The most usual subject for a cartoon was a political event, though any newsworthy topic could give rise to this treatment. Cartoons are often associated with humour, and are sometimes a devastating satire on their subject, but neither humour nor satire are essential. The clear, simplified format can be used without humour or irony to draw attention to crises and tragedies in a very thought provoking manner.

Cartoonists often employ caricature when they are depicting well-known people, with facial features deliberately exaggerated. A large nose becomes enormous and a receding chin may all but disappear. A figure can be clothed in a manner that suggests some characteristic, or the drawing might contain an object that has a negative connotation in the viewer's mind. There may be a few well-chosen words included in the sketch to give it context. As cartoons made no pretence of artistic veracity, they could be a medium for expressing sentiments that would have been difficult to put into words and might have invited a libel claim. Whilst the message is clear to an informed viewer, it is virtually impossible for someone who is being lampooned in a drawing to define

A Cartoon in The Walsall Advertiser 25th July 1908 shows the Prime Minister struggling to manage the economic problems of the day amidst increased demands for money. (*Courtesy of The British Newspaper Archive*)

exactly how the picture harmed their reputation, without digging themselves into a very deep hole.

Cartoons are often subversive in approach, which makes them an excellent source of information for historians. They show how informed journalists regarded key issues and figures in public life and may reveal a pattern of thought which differed from official pronouncements. Cartoons derived their legitimacy by reflecting what many people outside the establishment really thought of a situation, even if they had no way of making their views heard.

A development of the cartoon that commented on a political or official situation was one which commented on life in general, by taking a topical issue and offering a wry observation. The weather, cancelled trains and sporting events have all received this treatment. If a topic was the subject of a cartoon, a historian can accept that many people in the country were talking about it at that time.

Using Illustrated Sources

Most people find that pictures help to give context to a piece of research and some subjects are much easier to understand when pictures are available. Fashion is one of these and detailed drawings of the next season's styles were regularly included in magazines and newspapers, sometimes with instructions and diagrams for making them at home. Places too have been sketched and photographed and family historians should be able to discover what a town, village or possibly even the family home looked like when an ancestor lived there. Local historians may be able to track change and development through pictures.

Portraits in newspapers can sometimes surprise a researcher, as a person may appear unattractive, even though their looks were described in fulsome terms. Perceptions of beauty or handsomeness change over time. In this context, pictures can give a very practical demonstration of what a bygone age meant by particular words.

By the latter decades of the nineteenth century, illustrations in newspapers and magazines were abundant. At present only a small amount of this material is available on-line. Some has not been digitised and some has been lodged with commercial picture libraries which manage reproduction rights. A researcher who is searching for a specific image may have to refer to paper copies in a public archive or check with the commercial libraries.

Copyright and Reproduction Rights

An illustration or report from an old newspaper or magazine can enliven any piece of writing but anyone planning to include this type of material in a project, report, publication or on a website must establish whether they need permission to do so. The rules about reproducing old visual material are complicated. Initially, a researcher has to discover whether it is still covered by copyright and this can be difficult to establish. Always consult an official source, such as a government web site, to determine what the rules are rather than relying on someone's advice, unless they are professionally competent to give it. Also take care when sourcing images from websites and if they claim to be copyright free make sure this is really the case before using them. Even when material is out-of-copyright it may not be possible to use it without permission, unless an original copy is owned by the person who is reproducing it. Responsibility for ensuring that someone else's rights are not being infringed rests with the person who wants to use the material.

Conclusion

Newspaper illustrations are important historical sources for several reasons. They can show what a place, a person, or an event was like in a way that words cannot and may contain detail that a writer would have overlooked. They enable a historian to see what another audience saw and perhaps empathise. Old images also reveal the cultural values of the period when they were printed. The variety of subject matter depicted from the early years of illustrated newspapers shows there was willing audience for both high-minded and scandalous material alike. Pictures have many nuances and, with close study, they can disclose much more information than might be gleaned by a cursory glance.

Chapter 14

Using Newspapers with other Sources

What makes old newspapers unique is that they focussed on the present and captured detail at the point when a matter was in the public eye. Unless more information became available, journalists moved on to the next breaking sensation with barely a backward glance, often leaving loose ends in their wake. Despite the breadth and range of material newspapers contain, they offer only part of the evidence a historian needs and it is unwise to use them in isolation (unless they are the only source) or regard them as a short-cut or replacement source. A researcher who confines an investigation to newspapers alone risks producing work riddled with avoidable weaknesses. Researchers who try to investigate the past through newspapers alone are likely to encounter some of the following problems.

Antecedents

Historians often want to understand why an event occurred. Whilst the immediate cause of an incident can sometimes be found in a newspaper, in many cases a range of longer-term factors also contributed to it. News reports rarely make links between something that happened in the past and the current news. A change in the law, an economic recession, a technological advance, an influential book or a change in social attitudes may all help to explain why an event happened. Although newspapers may have reported these in a different context, researchers usually need to know what they are looking for in order to find information about antecedents. This makes it unlikely that newspapers will disclose the full range of factors that need to be considered to a researcher who has no prior knowledge of the subject.

Brick Walls

There are many news stories where newspaper coverage stops part way through. Examples include court cases that were adjourned and police investigations that were inconclusive.

Completeness

No newspaper report is ever likely to be a complete account of a situation as reporters had to communicate the essential elements of a story succinctly, perhaps in just a few hundred words. Detail they considered peripheral was rarely included so it is possible that some relevant information never became part of the news.

Lack of Information

Newspapers are not necessarily definitive sources. Editors could only report what they knew; if something was not known, it could not be included. Even though a newspaper may have reported in good faith, it may not have reflected the situation accurately.

Specific Incidents

Newspapers usually reported a number of individual incidents in isolation as they happened and did not necessarily try to reach wider conclusions about an issue. Even if they did, the breadth or complexity of the situation may not have been completely identified at the time. Researchers may need to analyse separate cases rather than relying on a single contemporary article or editorial.

Retrospective View

As well as considering the causes of an event, historians usually assess its long-term consequences. Newspapers rarely reflect on a topic from the past and when they do the short space available in the paper means that any analysis might be superficial or partial. If a periodical has considered the matter, it may have produced an analysis with more depth.

Other Sources for Historians

There are plenty of primary and secondary sources that a researcher can use in conjunction with old newspapers. Researchers who find it difficult to visit an archive may be able to access old documents and publications from home by searching the internet. Out-of-copyright books and official reports can sometimes be found in a digital format. University libraries, a website run by an official organisation, or a website run by someone with an interest in a topic are sources to investigate.

A number of organisations in the UK and other countries have digitised records about aspects of criminal justice, the armed forces, emigration and occupations making it possible to trace individuals. These can be an excellent resource for breaking down brick walls where newspaper coverage petered out before the end of a story.

Primary Sources

Primary sources were created at the time an event occurred and many of these would not have been available to contemporary newspapers. Government papers are normally kept private for at least thirty years and other records might have been created with no thought of publication. Influential politicians and ordinary people may have written notes, letters or diaries that reveal their role in an event or give an eye witness account of an incident. Those involved in a court case could have kept the paperwork for years and some of the lawyers who advised them later deposited their files with an archive. Some school, hospital and police records have survived from the nineteenth century and, subject to data protection issues, may be available to consult.

Primary source material is valuable. It can provide breadth where a newspaper has summarised, supply additional detail and perhaps offer a new perspective on what happened, how and why.

Secondary Sources

Secondary sources were created after an event, usually to interpret a situation. Some of these are much more authoritative than others and, when there is a multitude of secondary material and not enough time to check it all, consider the author's credentials when deciding which ones to focus on. If someone who was involved in a specific event published their own interpretation in a book, article, interview or autobiography, it is always worth reading.

Many topics already have their own secondary literature which has been produced over a period of years. Sometimes the secondary literature is as old, or almost as old, as the topic being investigated. The value of secondary sources is to see how others have approached the subject and the conclusions they have drawn. Secondary sources can help a researcher to clarify their thoughts and perhaps avoid reinventing the wheel. There is no merit in filling in an apparent gap if someone else has already found the answer. Secondary sources can also help identify if further research would be beneficial. When most of the secondary sources are old ones it might suggest that the topic is ripe for reappraisal.

If the secondary literature is out-of-print it may be difficult to find a copy. Second-hand bookshops may be able to help, as might websites but prices can sometimes be prohibitively high. Given sufficient notice, a public library should be able to make a copy available, though it might be on the premises rather than through a loan.

Oral History

If an event is within living memory, talking to those who can remember it may produce much richer material than is printed in any newspaper. Some archives have been recording memories from older people for many years and now hold good collections of taped material, so it may be possible to go back into the nineteenth century.

Some reports that have appeared in newspapers relate to personal rather than public matters. It may be possible to fill in gaps by speaking to someone who was around at the time, even if they were not directly involved. With the passage of years, and if no-one would be hurt, some people may be prepared to elaborate. Memorable stories tend to be passed down at least one generation in families, so it could be possible to discover new material from someone who had not been born when an incident occurred.

Conclusion

Digitised historical newspapers are perhaps the most exciting source of the twenty-first century and researchers are only just beginning to tap their potential. They are already yielding new insights into the past and offering different and innovative ways of investigating. Whatever information lies in their fascinating pages, a researcher who combines newspapers with all the other available sources is likely to produce the most rounded work and obtain the greatest satisfaction for a job well done.

A Study in Slander

A fictionalised Historical Investigation demonstrating points covered in Chapters 9-12.

This study is intended to give ideas for carrying out an investigation. It is not prescriptive as each researcher must decide what data to collect, how to record it, what analyses to carry out and how to develop their study.

In the nineteenth century, reputations were taken seriously and cases of slander were regularly taken to court. In order to gain an initial understanding of the issues involved, an analysis of all the cases heard at the Assizes for one county, Barsetshire, in 1876 was carried out.

Methodology Used

Step 1

A method for locating the cases and obtaining data was devised. The Barsetshire Assizes were held in March and July 1876 and the three newspapers that seemed most likely to include these cases were reviewed for the six weeks after the Assizes opened.

- The Allingham Post (the most important weekly newspaper in the county).
- The Barchester Chronicle, (an evening paper serving the town where the Assizes were held).
- The Barsetshire Echo (a daily newspaper serving the county).

Spreadsheet 1 shows the information that has been obtained about the fourteen cases which were heard.

The amount of detail available for each case varies.

A Study in Slander - Spreadsheet 1

Date	Source	Name	Damages	Age	Gender	Occupation	Reason	Additional Information
11/03/76	Bar Chron 13/3	Bridget	£50.00	32		Parlour maid	Hit a colleague	
12/03/76	Bar Chron 13/3	Desmond Clara	£200.00	21	M	Dau of Gentleman	Not given	Al Post 23. Bar Echo 21
15/03/76	Al Post 19/3	Popenjoy	£100.00					No other detail given
15/03/76	Al Post 19/3	James Miss	£1.00	60	F	Runs boarding house	Accused of stealing	
15/03/76	Bar Chron 18/3	Graham Lucy	£200.00	35		Governess	Alleged levity of manner	
16/03/76	Al Post 19/3	Desmoulines Madelaine	£0.00	28	F		Lost case	Madalina Demolines?
18/03/76	Al Post 19/3	Gerratty Norah	£25.00	26			Alleged levity of manner	Query spelling
19/03/76	Bar Chron 22/3	Proudie Mrs	£100.00		F		Arrogance	Married for 32 years
20/03/76	Al Post 26/3	Gresham Frances	£100.00				Insolvent	All 3 sources inconsistent
03/07/76	Bar Echo 6/7	Thorne Mary	£150.00			Dau of Gentleman	Said to be illegitimate	
04/07/76	Bar Echo 6/7	Wade George	£80.00		M	Servant		
05/07/76	Al Post 8/7	Dale Lily	£200.00			Independent Means	Said to be fickle	
06/07/76	Al Post 8/7	Crawley Josiah	£1,600.00	55		Vicar	Accused of stealing	
06/07/76	Bar Chron 10/8	Crosby Adolphus	£50.00		M	Shopkeeper	Social climbing	Not in other papers

A spreadsheet with grid lines.

Data Collection

Step 2

- Check Spreadsheet 1 to ensure that all entries seem reasonable.
- Clara Desmond is recorded as male which is incorrect.
- The damages of £1 to Miss James and £1,600 to Josiah Crawley are extremes, though not impossible awards. Ensure that sources agree on these amounts and that they have not been misread or a wrong figure typed in.

Step 3

- Decide whether any missing detail can be inferred.
- The gender of Bridget, Lucy Graham, Norah Gerratty, Mary Thorne, Lily Dale and Josiah Crawley can be established from their name, occupation or both.
- Mrs Proudie has been married for thirty-two years. Based on this and the fact that many women married when they were around twenty it is reasonable to infer that she is probably in her fifties.

Step 4

- Decide which missing detail (if any) is worth pursuing.
- It is unlikely that Bridget's surname, the forenames of Miss James or Mrs Proudie or confirming the spellings of Madelaine Desmoulines and Norah Gerratty would add anything relevant. There is a small discrepancy about Clara Desmond's age but resolving this is not expected to add anything to the investigation. All of these points can be followed up later in the study if they become significant.
- More detail about the cases of Clara Desmond, Popenjoy and George Wade would be useful as would Mrs Proudie's and Madelaine Desmoulines occupation (if any).
- The information about Frances Gresham should be collated to find what the sources agree on.

As Barsetshire has two other newspapers with a small circulation it would be appropriate to check these.

A Study in Slander – Spreadsheet 2

Date	Source	Name	Damages	Age	Gender	Occupation	Reason	Additional Information
11/03/76	Bar Chron 13/3	Bridget	£50.00	32	F	Parlour maid	Hit a colleague	
12/03/76	Bar Chron 13/3	Desmond Clara	£200.00	21	F	Dau of Gentleman	Not given	2 of 4 sources give age as 23
15/03/76	Al Post 19/3	Popenjoy	£100.00					3 sources have identical report
15/03/76	Al Post 19/3	James Miss	£1.00	60	F	Runs boarding house	Accused of stealing	
15/03/76	Bar Chron 18/3	Graham Lucy	£200.00	35	F	Governess	Alleged levity of manner	
16/03/76	Al Post 19/3	Desmoulines Madelaine	£0.00	28	F		Lost case	Madalina Demolines?
18/03/76	Al Post 19/3	Gerratty Norah	£25.00	26	F	Barmaid	Alleged levity of manner	Query spelling
19/03/76	Bar Chron 22/3	Proudie Mrs	£100.00	52	F		Arrogance	Married for 32 years. Age inferred
20/03/76	Al Post 26/3	Gresham Francis (Frank)	£100.00		M	Gentleman	Insolvent	Collated three sources
03/07/76	Bar Echo 6/7	Thorne Mary	£150.00		F	Dau of Gentleman	Said to be illegitimate	
04/07/76	Bar Echo 6/7	Wade George	£80.00		M	Servant	Incompetence	Extra info Silverbridge Merc 9/7
05/07/76	Al Post 8/7	Dale Lily	£200.00		F	Independent Means	Said to be fickle	
06/07/76	Al Post 8/7	Crawley Josiah	£1,600.00	55	M	Vicar	Accused of stealing	
06/07/76	Bar Chron 10/8	Crosby Adolphus	£50.00		M	Shopkeeper	Social climbing	Not in other papers

Notes
Italics Do not use this detail if age is analysed in detail rather than by age band

A spreadsheet without grid lines. Turning off grid lines before printing can aid presentation.

Step 5

- Steps 2-4 have identified 7 genders, 1 reason and 1 error. They have inferred 1 age and put 1 age in doubt, but not significantly. Spreadsheet 2 incorporates all of this new information.
- As all the information available from the five local newspapers has been obtained, consider whether national publications or those from outside Barsetshire would yield any outstanding detail. Josiah Crawley's case would probably be found in many other papers. Several of the others may have been reported elsewhere.
- An electronic query would reveal whether Clara Desmond, Mrs Proudie and Popenjoy were covered more widely. Use wildcards with Popenjoy's name as it is unusual and could have been mis-spelt.
- When these checks have been made it would be reasonable to conclude that no further detail is available.
- Decide whether there is enough information about Popenjoy to include the case in analyses. As the damages are known there is information to use in connection with averages and frequency which justifies keeping it in the sample.

Step 6

Spreadsheet 3 shows the cases sorted by highest to lowest damages so that averages can be calculated. Separating Madelaine Desmoulines who lost her case prevents it becoming entangled with the successful ones.

Averages

The spreadsheet can be used to calculate the mean average damages. This is £2,856 /13 = £219.69

The mean average is higher than all but one award of damages and reveals that the distribution is affected by an extreme value.

As there were 13 successful cases the median average will be the middle (ie the 7th item from top and bottom.) This is Mrs Proudie who won £100.

Any of the claimants who won £100 could be used to study a mid-range case. The frequency of each award reveals the mode average. This is the sum awarded most times.

A Study in Slander – Spreadsheet 3

Date	Source	Name	Damages	Age	Gender	Occupation	Reason	Additional Information
06/07/76	Al Post 8/7	Crawley Josiah	£1,600.00	55	M	Vicar	Accused of stealing	
12/03/76	Bar Chron 13/3	Desmond Clara	£200.00	21	F	Dau of Gentleman	Not given	2 of 4 sources give age as 23
15/03/76	Bar Chron 18/3	Graham Lucy	£200.00	35	F	Governess	Alleged levity of manner	
05/07/76	Al Post 8/7	Dale Lily	£200.00		F	Independent Means	Said to be fickle	
03/07/76	Bar Echo 6/7	Thorne Mary	£150.00		F	Dau of Gentleman	Said to be illegitimate	
15/03/76	Al Post 19/3	Popenjoy	£100.00					3 sources have identical report
19/03/76	Bar Chron 22/3	Proudie Mrs	£100.00	52	F		Arrogance	Married for 32 years. Age inferred
20/03/76	Al Post 26/3	Gresham Francis (Frank)	£100.00		M	Gentleman	Insolvent	Collated three sources
04/07/76	Bar Echo 6/7	Wade George	£80.00		M	Servant	Incompetence	Extra Info Silverbridge Merc 9/7
11/03/76	Bar Chron 13/3	Bridget	£50.00	32	F	Parlour maid	Hit a colleague	
06/07/76	Bar Chron 10/8	Crosby Adolphus	£50.00		M	Shopkeeper	Social climbing	Not in other papers
18/03/76	Al Post 19/3	Gerratty Norah	£25.00	26	F	Barmaid	Alleged levity of manner	Query spelling
15/03/76	Al Post 19/3	James Miss	£1.00	60	F	Runs boarding house	Accused of stealing	
		Total damages	£2,856.00					
		Mean average damages	£219.69					
16/03/76	Al Post 19/3	Desmoulines Madelaine	£0.00	28	F		Lost case	Madalina Demolines?

Notes

Italics Do not use this detail if age is analysed in detail rather than by age band

A spreadsheet without grid lines.

Sum	frequency
£1,600	1
£200	3
£150	1
£100	3
£80	1
£50	2
£25	1
£1	1
	13

There are two sums which were awarded the most often, £100 and £200. Considering similarities and differences between the two sets of cases may produce valuable insights.

Work out other important characteristics of the data, including totals as a check that nothing has been omitted or double-counted. Think about what the characteristics could represent, if anything.

Success and Failure

13 cases succeeded
 1 case failed
14

This is a success rate of 93 per cent which seems very high. Was it usual? As the person who lost the case has a foreign sounding name, could her nationality have had a bearing on the outcome?

Age

3	21–30
2	31–40
3 (1 inferred)	51–60
6	unknown
14	

There is too much missing data to suggest any lines of enquiry.

Gender

9 cases were brought by females
4 cases were brought by males
<u>1</u> case gender not known
<u>14</u>

Women brought approximately twice as many cases as men. Was this typical?

Occupation of Successful Claimants

4 no need to work (Clara Desmond, Lily Dale, Mary Thorne, Francis Gresham)
2 servants (Bridget, George Wade)
1 clergyman (Josiah Crawley)
1 governess (Lucy Graham)
3 engaged in trade (Norah Gerratty, Adolphus Crosby, Miss James)
<u>2</u> not known (Popenjoy, Mrs Proudie)
<u>13</u>

Although some data is missing it appears that claimants range from having 'no financial need to work' to 'working class'.

Reason for Successful Claims

2 accused of stealing
2 levity of manner
1 fickle
1 illegitimate
1 arrogant
1 insolvent
1 incompetent
1 violent
1 social climber
<u>2</u> not given
<u>13</u>

Consider whether any of this could be grouped. For example, being fickle, arrogant, violent, light of manner or a social climber are personal characteristics. Being illegitimate or insolvent are factual situations.

Step 7

Start to consider what the data means.

- There are 4 instances of damages greater than £150, and 9 instances of damages of up to £150. This suggests that the majority of slander victims do not receive excessively high compensation.
- It is striking that the highest and lowest damages were awarded to someone accused of stealing, a serious crime. The damages awarded to Josiah Crawley seem exceptionally high, relative to the next highest award which was £200. This suggests that there may be something very unusual about this case.
- Similarly the damages awarded to Miss James seem very low, especially as Adolphus Crosby obtained £50 for a much less serious accusation, social climbing. This suggests that the damages awarded to Miss James were influenced by considerations other than that she was wrongly accused of committing a crime.
- Miss James and Mr Crawley were of a similar age, so this may not be relevant. They were of a different gender which may be a factor, especially in view of the damages awarded to Adolphus Crosby.
- Checking the fine detail of the cases of Miss James and Josiah Crawley may point to a possible explanation. A clergyman's reputation could be seriously damaged by the suggestion that he had broken one of the Ten Commandments and his livelihood lost. Boarding house keepers were sometimes considered to be brothel keepers, so their reputation would suffer much less from an imputation of dishonesty. Perhaps Miss James had been convicted for theft in the past and spent time in prison. In such a case a jury may not let her profit from being falsely accused on this occasion. Perhaps the allegation about Josiah Crawley had been made maliciously with the intention of forcing him to resign from his parish. In such a situation the jury would probably award exemplary damages because of the other party's bad conduct.
- There is also a disparity between the damages given to Lucy Graham and Norah Gerratty for the same slander, levity of manner. As both were women of a similar age and social standing the difference may lie in occupation. A

governess who was accused of levity of manner could find her employment prejudiced. A barmaid would not suffer this disadvantage.

- Noticeably, the three ladies of high social standing, Clara Desmond, Lily Dale and Mary Thorne received £200 or £150. Has their status led a jury to be more generous to them than to a poorer woman or does it reflect the values prevailing in 1876?
- Two servants were awarded damages. Bridget obtained £50 for a false allegation that she was violent. George Wade won £80 for alleged incompetence. Does this reflect the values of the time towards these two slanders or could the difference relate to gender?
- Some insight may arise from the mean average of the damages awarded to males and females (though excluding both Mr Crawley and Miss James to whose awards very individual factors applied). The men (Gresham, Wade, Crosby) average £76.67. The women (Desmond, Graham, Dale, Thorne, Proudie, Bridget, Gerratty) averaged £132.14. This suggests that there had been no gender discrimination in favour of men. It raises the question of whether females were treated more favourably than men.

The number of items in this study is far too small to support any definite conclusions about the claim for slander. Analysing the data, thinking about what it might mean and being aware of the background of 1876 has indicated some possible lines of future enquiry, including:

- Did allegations that could adversely affect someone's ability to earn their living lead to better levels of damages than those that did not?
- Was slander affecting a genteel woman considered more serious than slander of a poor woman?
- Did women receive higher damages than men unless the slander seriously affected a man's reputation?
- The success rate seems very high. Why did just one case fail?

Keeping these points in mind, if the study is extended, is acceptable practice. It would be unacceptable to exploit this data to reach a desired conclusion by, for example, ensuring that the additional examples were ones where men received low damages and women received high ones.

Step 8

Other points to consider

- Converting the damages to current day values will provide information about what the awards would have been worth to the claimant in 1876. This may offer insight about why some people took a case to court.
- Comparing the damages awarded for slander with those awarded for other civil claims may provide insight about what was considered serious or less serious in 1876.
- Might age might be relevant to understanding the claim? If this seems an important element, find a way of locating as much outstanding data as possible. On-line birth records may be helpful.
- Would information about the defendants in these cases add depth? If so, decide whether to backtrack and collect it.
- If the study is to be extended would it be sensible to include the reason why a claim was unsuccessful?
- Would assigning a code to some aspects of the study be helpful? If it is to be extended or repeated, codes to represent the reason for the case and social standing of those involved could be devised.
- Reading more widely about the most significant cases in the study in other newspapers may provide more context. Editorial could reveal how the case was perceived at the time.
- Which claims make good case studies? The most representative cases will be those surrounding the median average of £100. The most interesting cases or those with the most detail may be Josiah Crawley, Miss James and Madelaine Desmoulines, none of which are representative as two won exceptional damages and the third was the only claim to fail.
- Is further information about slander required and are newspapers the best source? Would a modern law textbook or a law treatise written in the mid-nineteenth century or a combination of these have more to offer?

Step 9

If this is a complete study in itself, consider how to write it up and whether graphs would be helpful. If the spreadsheet is to be printed out, remember that the grid lines can be switched off which can improve presentation.

Step 10

There are a number of ways in which the study could be developed. Choosing another cluster sample (or samples) would be a good approach because it would prevent bias from influencing the items being selected.

- Repeat the same study for counties adjacent to Barsetshire for 1876. This will help to ascertain whether the same factors applied throughout the region.
- Repeat the study for counties with similar socio-economic characteristics to Barsetshire for 1876. This will help ascertain what similarities applied across Britain.
- Repeat the study for counties with different socio-economic characteristics to Barsetshire for 1876. This will help to identify whether slander was regarded in the same manner in highly industrial and less industrial locations.
- Extend the study in Barsetshire by looking at 1877 and then 1878. This will help to identify how typical the results for Barsetshire in 1876 were.
- Look at change over time by checking the position in Barsetshire every third year. Repeat this study for any other areas that have been investigated in 1876.
- Expand the study by investigating cases of libel heard at the Barsetshire Assizes in 1876. This will provide information about two aspects of defamation.

Every time the study is extended, so long as enough examples are included, it will provide data that should help to confirm, refine or refute the hypotheses that developed from the initial investigation.

Instead of extending the study, the investigation may suggest other research topics:

- Investigating the attitudes towards clergymen in the Victorian age.
- Ascertaining whether a woman's social class and gender had any bearing on how she was treated when taking action in the civil courts.
- If information about Miss James or Madelaine Desmoulines is available it may be possible to reconstruct their life story and shed light on social attitudes.

Research from Newspaper Sources

Nine Case Studies

The following nine examples show some of the practical ways researchers are using historical newspapers to shed light on the past.

Challenging Established Ideas

Denise Bates

Two eminent academics gave huge prominence to the death of a gingerbread vendor who was kicked to death by a mob at Stalybridge Wakes in 1850. George Kitson Clark recounted the story in a lecture in 1960 and included it in *The Making of Victorian England*. In 1961, Edward Carr discussed it in his book, *What is History?* as he analysed why some facts pass into history and others fade into oblivion.

The Stalybridge Wakes murder features in *Seventy Years a Showman*, the memoirs of circus owner George Sanger, first published in 1910. Sanger was specific about the time and place because it was the day he heard of the death of his father, James who died in 1850. In the 1980s, an amateur historian from Stalybridge failed to find any other source to corroborate this, despite a thorough trawl of available local newspapers and other records.

Digitised newspapers now provide wide-ranging and powerful tools. Thirty years on, I searched again but still found no reports of this murder at Stalybridge Wakes in any year. I expected a violent death at a local wakes to be reported by at least one paper so I checked many years of newspapers countrywide, thinking it possible that Sanger's memory had blurred in sixty years.

So far I have discovered no corroboration of Sanger's account either in Stalybridge or elsewhere. Unless independent evidence of Sanger's story is found, the murder at Stalybridge Wakes can no longer be regarded as a fact.

Establishing the Contemporary Position

Suzie Grogan

As a writer and researcher on the subject of mental health and history, and being commissioned to write a book about the impact of the First World War on the mental health of the nation, I was keen to offer original material and look at the stress of war through fresh eyes, seeing events through the perspective of contemporary news reports. I turned to the columns digitised at *The British Newspaper Archive* online.

I discovered that although much of the news was subject to censorship during the war, there were still graphic descriptions of the horrors faced on the Home Front as German Zeppelins and Gotha aircraft bombed towns and cities for example. *Shell Shocked Britain* looks at how far the nation as a whole was 'shell shocked' by the impact of the conflict, and the aftermath (including the Spanish influenza outbreak), and how a generation of men, women and children, for whom unspeakable horrors, grief, loss and anxiety became the norm, coped. The newspapers, examined with a recognition of their agenda at the time, offered some of the clearest information about life during and after the First World War. *Shell Shocked Britain* would be a less interesting book had such a wide variety of sources not be available to me.

Suzie Grogan's book *Shell Shocked Britain: The First World War's legacy for Britain's mental health* is published by Pen and Sword Books.

Confirming Oral History

Denise Bates

My Grandfather-in-law, who was born in Barnsley in 1896, always said that as a baby he had met James Kier Hardie, the first leader of the Labour party, but he had no further details. It was not an impossible contention, given that he had Scottish ancestors and his father had been a Labour Councillor but, without knowing more about the circumstances, it was difficult to envisage when the meeting could have happened.

A newspaper obituary of his father provided the answer. When a parliamentary seat in Barnsley became vacant in September 1897 the Independent Labour Party, then in its infancy, fielded its first candidate in a by-election, believing that a vacancy in a mining area was one which a working man could win.

Leading figures in the party, including Keir Hardie, visited the town and asked the Trades Council to support the Gas Workers' union leader, Peter Curran as their candidate. It is likely that my Great-Grandfather-in-law, who had been an active member of the Barnsley Trades Council for several years, was at the meeting which Hardie and Curran attended. He certainly took a prominent role in Curran's by-election campaign in the town.

Whilst this visit is not conclusive proof that my Grandfather-in-law did meet the Labour Party leader as a baby, it demonstrates that there was an opportunity for such a meeting. In conjunction with the oral history, it is reasonable to conclude that the pair did meet.

Validating Other Sources

Angela Buckley

My primary source for researching the work of Detective Jerome Caminada was his memoirs. I used other source material, such as contemporary newspapers, to validate his accounts and add supplementary detail. Many of Detective Caminada's cases were recorded in the local press, particularly the trials.

I selected publications that would give the closest description of actual events: the *Manchester Courier*, *Manchester Evening News* and the *Manchester Guardian*. I then checked reports of the same event in other regional and national publications. The main challenge was the differing accounts, which sometimes contradicted Caminada's recollections. I overcame this by reconstructing specific cases step-by-step, working my way through records of investigations and trials, whilst bearing in mind Caminada's own reminiscences. I tried to remain as close as possible to the statements of those present at the event, even if their viewpoints differed slightly. Often the different versions gave a more comprehensive insight into a single incident.

In addition, I discovered new information in the newspaper articles that had been missing from the primary sources. One of Detective Caminada's most famous cases, the cross-dressing ball, was widely reported in the press, including the *Illustrated Police News*, but was omitted from his memoirs.

Contemporary newspapers yielded new leads for further research, colourful detail and an external view of Detective Caminada. First hand accounts of his cases, physical descriptions, transcriptions of his depositions in court and his obituaries gave me fresh insight into his personal characteristics, which were essential to writing his biography.

Angela Buckley's biography of Jerome Caminada, *The Real Sherlock Holmes*, is published by Pen and Sword Books.

Building a Community History

Denise Bates

I became interested in Jarratts Buildings whilst researching my family history. The name refers to fifty-four back-to-back dwellings built in Worsbrough Dale in 1858 to house workers at a local colliery and which were finally demolished in 1957. I realised there was a community history to be understood, across a pivotal century of change, not just the lives of three generations of my ancestors.

No-one had ever put together a history of *the fifty four*, although incidental references to it are scattered in local histories, council records and in family trees available on the internet. I started to pull together any details I could find. Censuses gave valuable insights as did parish registers but they lacked the human element. I suspected there was a wealth of information preserved in local newspapers about the residents, but at that point Barnsley papers had to be searched on microfilm and, not living locally, this was impractical.

The British Newspaper Archive was key to progressing the project. I could search on-line for residents and the buildings. Even without the Barnsley titles there was enough detail in papers from Leeds and Sheffield to give the project critical mass. I was able to post to my website and offer talks. This generated interest and information from others who had family histories in Jarratts. Newspapers proved a vital tool for unlocking the oral sources that transformed my study into a project about a community rather than just its buildings.

Discovering a Cover-Up

Gill Hoffs

When researching RMS *Tayleur*, which wrecked off the Irish coast in 1854, I gathered most of the information I needed from searchable online news. This enabled me to draw new conclusions as to the cause, including a theory regarding the captain's unusual behaviour.

It seemed clear from accounts of the inquiries there had been a cover-up, which is why – despite the tragedy making newspapers around the world – few know of it today. But it was only when I found a journalist's scathing remark, bemoaning the difficulties of working for a newspaper, that I discovered this clipper's fatal flaws were known before 700 people set sail for the Australian Gold Rush … and that journalists were forced to keep quiet!

Old newspapers are deliciously gossipy and often give details about people, places, or events that can only be guessed at today. In a time before photos appeared in the press, I was delighted to read an advert for the initially anonymous orphan known as the "Ocean Child", which helped reunite the baby with his grandmother and allowed me to describe him as a clingy baby with blue eyes and curly blond hair.

Comparing the variances in names and ages in passenger lists helped me trace descendants through family trees and also find other articles on them, including an ex-convict called Samuel Carby/Kirby/Carley who was a handsome hero and romantic too. At first he was impossible to trace but once I found the alternative spellings there was plenty to learn and I've since met his great-great-grandson.

Gill Hoffs' book *The Sinking of RMS Tayleur: The Lost Story of the 'Victorian Titanic'* is published by Pen and Sword Books.

Providing New Insights

Denise Bates

By the twenty-first century, the former legal claim for breach of promise to marry was regarded with derision. The concept of a woman demanding financial compensation from the man who had jilted her is alien to modern values and the archaic law had already receded into obscurity. After chancing upon a different case almost every time I looked at an old newspaper, I realised that the claim had little to do with lost love, but just how did it fit into the wider social fabric?

Newspapers are the best source of information about breach of promise cases as papers from very few claims have survived in archives. Reports of court hearings contain similar details, so I was able to extract extensive information including the age, occupation, social class and damages awarded and enter them into a spreadsheet. This made it possible to discover what the claim meant and how it had changed over time. I made several new and unexpected discoveries, including the fact that breach of promise had been used for over a century to give women indirect remedies against a former fiancé when they lacked direct remedies under property or child maintenance law.

This study was possible because I could locate cases by using the search term 'breach of promise', which meant that I could be reasonably sure that I had not missed anything significant. It also found editorial and opinion articles about breach of promise, which helped with interpreting my results.

The Unexpected Discovery

Denise Bates

I wanted the example graphs in this book to relate to some aspect of the past. I knew that in *The Go-Between,* LP Hartley's wonderful novel, the young narrator recorded the daily temperatures in his diary during his visit to Norfolk in July 1900. The action of the story is reflected in the changing weather over nineteen days. *The Times* contained the actual temperatures for those dates and I extracted this data to use as the basis of my graphs.

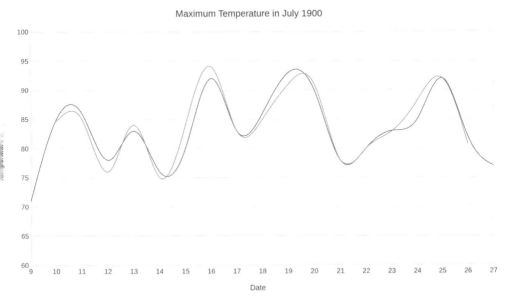

Maximum Temperature in July 1900

Unable to resist the urge to re-read the novel I noted down all the temperatures as they were mentioned. To my amazement they were very close to the ones recorded in *The Times*, as shown by this graph which compares the two.

My admiration for Hartley the author, already high, has increased immeasurably with this discovery. His plot could equally well have been set in August, the zodiac sign of Leo, and many lesser writers would have taken this option. Instead, Hartley identified three weeks that could provide a meticulously accurate background for his story and crafted a masterpiece of fiction within the confines of fact. Without old newspapers I would have remained in ignorance of this piece of virtuosity.

How Newspapers Reported Conflict

Rachel Bates

The role of newspapers and journalists has been a crucial aspect of my research on British responses to the Crimean War (1854-1856). This war, largely remembered for the Charge of the Light Brigade and Florence Nightingale, inaugurated 'Special Correspondents' who reported from the front. It also saw the repeal of Newspaper Stamp Duty, known as the 'tax on knowledge', on 30 June 1855. The latter development resulted in cheaper issues and an increase in the number of newspaper publications. Prominent peace campaigners – Joseph Sturge, Richard Cobden and John Bright – established the *Morning Star* and *Evening Star* following the repeal of the tax, allowing them to challenge the pro-war views of mainstream newspapers.

The most widely circulated newspaper during the War was *The Times*, whose special correspondents, particularly William Howard Russell, provided detailed commentary of combat but also the conditions faced by the British Army on campaign. Journalists were treated with suspicion by Army headquarters as there were no rules governing the work of reporters in war zones at this time and military censorship was at the discretion of newspaper editors. It is therefore important to bear in mind the political agendas of newspapers and the selective acts of editors when researching public opinion, particularly in the heightened emotional climate of wartime. *The Times* supported its anti-establishment editorial policy by publishing letters from junior officers and the ranks expressing pessimistic views about supplies and strategy. Conversely, the conservative daily *The Morning Post* responded to this policy by only printing letters from relatively content soldiers. The Chartist and republican *Reynolds's Newspaper* was one of the few publications to denounce royal publicity stunts to restore faith in Army command and used every opportunity to lobby for promotion from the Army's ranks.

Rachel Bates recently completed an AHRC funded PhD entitled 'Curating the Crimea: The Cultural Afterlife of a Conflict', supervised by the University of Leicester and the National Army Museum. She has published articles in *The British Art Journal* and *19: Interdisciplinary Studies in the Long Nineteenth Century* on the Crimean War.

Appendix 1

Accessing Old Newspapers

On-line

The *Times*, *The Guardian* and *The Observer* are available to search free in major public libraries. If you are using them in the library, check access arrangements in advance as you may need to book a computer.

Many libraries make free access available to users in their own homes, at any time. You will be required to register with the library to obtain a password, and may have to provide identification. If your local library does not have a subscription that allows you remote access to these newspapers, it is usually possible to register as a user with a library in a town or city which does.

An increasing number of national, regional and local newspapers have been digitised by *The British Newspaper Archive* (www.britishnewspaperarchive. co.uk) and are available to subscribers in their own homes. Users have to take out a subscription either directly with *The British Newspaper Archive* or with a family history website such as *Find My Past*. Prices vary, and it is worth checking which provider will best meet your wider research needs before committing.

Educational institutions have subscriptions to a wide range of on-line media resources and may have access to *British Newspapers 1600-1900*. Staff and students of an educational establishment are usually able to use resources for free and some offer this to their registered alumni. It may be necessary to be on site to use them. Some resources used in the educational sector are not available to individual users or a subscription would be prohibitively expensive. Sometimes it is possible to purchase an individual article from the supplier.

If you really cannot obtain the information you require from any other source at a realistic price it may be worth approaching an institution and asking if you can use their facilities. They have no obligation to assist but serious researchers with a compelling case may be granted discretionary access.

On Microfilm

Local libraries and archives often hold microfilm copies of old newspapers relating to their area. These are usually available to consult on the premises. It is sensible to discuss requirements with an archive in advance rather than arriving on spec as it may be necessary to book a microfilm reader for your visit. Some archives have digitised their microfilm holdings so that they can be searched to some extent and viewed on a computer, but only on site. Archives generally require researchers to provide proof of identity before they are allowed to use the collections.

Printed Copies

Not all newspapers have been digitised or microfilmed and some only exist in a paper format. They may be available at a local archive or in the collection of the British Library. These newspapers are valuable and sometimes fragile. Users have to make specific arrangements with the holding institution to consult them.

Appendix 2

Worldwide Newspaper Websites

Many countries have old newspapers available on-line. They can be an excellent way of discovering the lives of emigrant ancestors. They are also a useful way of discovering how news about Britain was perceived in other parts of the world, as well as for researching the history of those countries. There may be a charge for accessing any newspaper.

There are a number of websites, some maintained by Universities, that post information about which papers are available on-line and possibly links to them. As new material is appearing on-line weekly, it is unlikely that any site can guarantee to be up-to-date, so it is worth checking more than one.

Sites which hold a considerable amount of material in English include:

http://www.chroniclingamerica.loc.gov – A project providing access to digitised newspapers from the United States.

http://trove.nla.gov.au – A National Library of Australia project giving access to newspapers and periodicals.

http://natlib.govt.nz – Papers Past is managed by the National Library of New Zealand.

http://libguides.bgsu.edu/CanadianNewspapers – provides links to Canadian newspapers that are freely available on-line.

https://www.irishnewsarchive.com/ – A subscription website for newspapers from Northern Ireland and the Irish Republic.

http://www.gutenberg.org – provides free downloads of out of copyright e-books. The site has some periodicals, including *Punch* and *Chambers Journal* available and is always worth checking.

https://news.google.com – contains a number of historical newspapers from many countries.

Sites holding material in languages other than English include:

http://gallica.bnf.fr/html/presse-et-revues/les-principaux-quotidiens –
   Information about historical newspapers from France.
http://www.ub.uni-bielefeld.de/diglib/aufklaerung/zeitschriften.htm –
   Information about historical newspapers from Germany.
http://welshnewspapers.llgc.org.uk – A site operated by the National Library
   of Wales, it holds some newspapers written in Welsh.

Appendix 3

Other Websites for Researchers

The following web sites may be a helpful starting point for information about the stated topic.

http://archiveshub.ac.uk/ – Information about searching for archives.

http://www.bl.uk/reshelp/findhelprestype/news/blnewscoll/ – information about the British Library's newspaper collections.

http://www.connectedhistories.org – A range of digital resources relating to early modern and nineteenth century Britain, including some British newspapers 1600–1900.

http://discovery.nationalarchives.gov.uk – Information about records held by the National Archives and other public archives.

http://www.freebmd.org.uk – Details of births, marriages and deaths in England and Wales 1837–1983.

https://www.gov.uk/using-somebody-elses-intellectual-property/copyright – Information about copyright and seeking permission to use such material.

http://www.hse.gov.uk/msd/dse/index.htm – The website of the Health and Safety Executive provides guidance about using computer equipment safety.

http://www.measuringworth.com – for ascertaining the current value of money.

http://www.metricconversions.org – for converting non-metric units to metric ones.

http://www.oldbaileyonline.org – access to information about trials held at the Old Bailey 1674-1913.

http://www.scotlandspeople.gov.uk/ – Details of births, marriages and deaths in Scotland.

Appendix 4

Money, Weights and Measures

Money

Until 1971 Britain did not use a decimal system and its currency was made up of pounds (£), shillings (s) and pence (d). The sign £ was placed before the number. The signs s and d were placed after the number.

£1   20s
1s   12d

There were 240 pennies in a pound.

A penny divided into half pennies and farthings (a quarter of a penny). The farthing ceased to be legal tender in 1960, and the half penny in 1969.

Some coins had official names. A two shilling piece was a florin and a half crown was worth 2s 6d. A crown was worth five shillings. A half sovereign was worth ten shillings and a sovereign was worth a pound. A guinea was worth £1 1s 0d.

Notes worth £1 and 10s were much more widely used than their coin versions of half sovereigns and sovereigns. Guineas were also comparatively rare as coins but prices, especially of luxury goods, were sometimes expressed in these terms.

There was more than one way of expressing a price in figures. Five shillings and seven pence could be written as 5s 7d or 5/7 or 5/7d. When spoken, the word shilling was usually omitted, making the amount five and seven or five and seven pence.

On occasions, prices were written as shillings and pence, even if their value was more than a pound. Two pounds and 15 shillings might also be expressed as 55 shillings, 55s, 55/0, 55/0d or 55/-.

A few coins and their values had unofficial names. Two pence was often expressed as tuppence and three pence could be thruppence. The coin worth three pence was known as threepenny bit. The coin worth six pence was known as a sixpence, or a tanner. The shilling piece was known as a shilling or a bob. The term groat to mean fourpence survived well into the nineteenth century, well after the groat coin was withdrawn from use.

When the decimal system was introduced, there were 100 new pence in a pound. The conversion of pre-decimal pennies was as follows:

1d	0.5p
2d	1.0p
3d	1.0p
4d	1.5p
5d	2.0p
6d	2.5p
7d	3.0p
8d	3.5p
9d	4.0p
10d	4.0p
11d	4.5p
12d	5.0p

When doing calculations involving pre-decimal currency it is often more practical to convert amounts into their decimal equivalent and then convert the answer back if it is necessary to express it in pre-decimal format. If you are using a spreadsheet, it will not be possible to use its calculation functions, unless values are in a currency format it recognises.

If amounts are converted to a modern £ p format, any sum of less than 2d cannot be expressed accurately. In practice it may not be necessary to achieve absolute precision and converting all values under 2d as £0.01 may be sufficient. If more accuracy is needed:

1d	£0.005
1/2d	£0.0025
1/4d	£0.00125

In this situation, it will be necessary to set a spreadsheet to a format that supports values to 5 decimal places.

Weights and Measures
Until the latter part of the twentieth century Britain used Imperial Weights and Measures. These have been superseded, rather than changed, in a manner similar to the change to decimal currency.

Weight and Volume
The main ones were ounce (oz) pound (lb), stone (st), hundredweight (cwt) and ton (ton).

16 oz	1 lb
14 lb	1 st
2 st	1 quarter
4 quarters	1 cwt
20 cwt	1 ton

For conversion purposes 1lb is 0.454kilograms. A metric tonne is close to an Imperial ton.
 The main measurements of fluid were pint (pt) quart (qt) and gallon (g or gal)

2 pts	1 qt
4 qts	1 gal

A gill was a quarter of a pint.
 For conversion purposes 1 pint is 0.568261 litres

Distance
The principal units of distance were inch (in), foot (ft), yard (yd), and mile (ml).

12 ins	1 ft
3 ft	1 yd
22 yds	1 chain
10 chains	1 furlong
8 furlongs	1 ml

For conversion purposes 1 yard is 0.9144 metres

Writing Up

If you are writing up research that involved pre-decimal currency, or Imperial weights and measures, consider the units you are using. Whilst the units of the time are technically more accurate, in practical terms they may not mean much to readers. Hardly anyone under fifty-five years old now remembers the nuances of pre-decimal currency, and many people under thirty have no understanding of the old weights and measures. If you opt to use the units of the time you may need to explain how they relate to metric units. If you choose to use metric units you should note why you have used this approach rather than the units of the time.

Appendix 5

Publicising Results

Some researchers will be keen to share their findings with a wider audience. There are opportunities available, but many of them are unpaid. Publicising research may involve direct costs such as paper and ink, indirect costs such as travelling expenses and time. If any of them have to be borne by the researcher, find out in advance what the costs are likely to be and decide whether you are prepared to incur them before committing to anything. Professional historians may find it easier to disseminate their research than amateur ones.

Printed Outlets

Book Publication may be appropriate if a study has discovered something ground-breaking or that could attract a wide audience. The best way forward is to consult *The Writers and Artists Yearbook* to identify potential publishers.

Specialist Journals for historians, or relevant to the topic of study, may be prepared to publish new research that has been carried out to a very high standard. Some of these journals require research to be written up in a certain manner, or to be peer reviewed. Some are likely to favour submissions from professional historians.

Newspapers and magazines are usually prepared to consider contributions from professional and amateur researchers and writers. There is plenty of competition and the topic needs to appeal to a wide audience to have a chance of acceptance.

Booklets may occasionally be financed by a grant-maker or organisation if a piece of research is original, high quality and relevant to the funder's objectives.

Pamphlets can be created and printed by a researcher who is able to use a Desktop Publishing programme.

Local and family history societies are usually happy to include articles in their magazines if the research is related to their area. Societies that cover a specialist topic may be interested in publishing new discoveries about it.

On-line Outlets

Websites can be created to publicise research. They are not unduly expensive for anyone who is able and prepared to develop and maintain them. A personal website may not be worthwhile if someone has to be paid for working on it. A further point to consider is how many people will find the site, or be sufficiently interested to read it.

Blogging (writing an article) for someone else's website is an option for a researcher who does not want a website of their own. There are several history websites with a good reputation and plenty of followers who are willing to host guest posts when the subject matter is relevant to their theme. These can be found by looking on-line. *The British Newspaper Archive* and some family and local history websites welcome guest posts from users.

Social Media pages can be set up for free on many sites. Subject to the provider's rules, these can be used to put research into the public domain.

Self Publishing an Electronic Book is feasible and some writers do so successfully. There is plenty of information on the internet about how to publish in E-reader format. It will be necessary for the researcher to typeset and proof read their own manuscript and there is no guarantee of sales.

Oral Outlets

Guest speakers are welcomed by many groups.

Community and local radio stations may be interested in a short talk or conducting an interview, when research is relevant to their area.

Conferences and literary festivals provide an opportunity to share findings with others. There is often strong competition for speaker slots and professional historians and writers have an advantage over amateur ones.

Other Outlets

Formal Accreditation

Universities and colleges may offer an accredited qualification that the research would count towards. Information about courses and qualifications can be found via the Internet.

Paid For Publication

Anyone who considers paying to publish their research must think very carefully from the outset about what they are doing and why. There are publishers who will print any book if the author pays all the associated costs. This is known as vanity publishing and some publishers make unrealistic promises about future sales to secure business. Vanity publishing often ends with the author substantially out-of-pocket. Reputable sales outlets do not stock books by vanity publishers and newspapers do not review them. If a piece of research has sales potential it will be possible to find a commercial publisher who will print it at their own expense.

Sometimes, a family historian wants to formalise their research in booklet form for their family, or members of a society might like a pamphlet that would have very limited appeal. In these situations, a researcher may decide to commission a book packager or printer. Always agree a price before committing and make sure that you can afford to pay it. If the book is to be sold to members of a group, check that everyone is happy with the price and, ideally, collect the money upfront. At an early stage, agree your expectations about quality and time scale with the publisher/printer and what is to happen if these are not met.

Glossary

History is usually categorised in types. For readers who are not familiar with the main classifications, the following provides a very brief outline of terms mentioned in this book.

Main Classifications

Political History:	relates to the way in which a country was governed
Economic History:	focusses on matters relating to wealth and prosperity of a place
Social History:	considers how people and communities lived

Sub-Classifications

Constitutional History:	studies the organisations of government
Cultural History:	focusses on how a society expresses itself through its art, music etc.
Family History:	studies matters concerning a group of related people
Foreign History:	relates to the history of a place other than the United Kingdom
Intellectual History:	relates to the development and spread of ideas
Legal History:	studies the development of law and how it operated
Local History:	relates to a small entity such as a town and its surrounding area
Military History:	relates to a country's armed forces and wars they fought

Further Reading

Historical Research Using British Newspapers has brought together information from a number of disciplines. Readers who wish to delve deeper into any of the topics covered in this book, may find the following suggestions a useful starting point.

History of the Press in Great Britain

This is a very wide subject, spanning over three centuries. Information about it can be found in a number of places, including the internet. There are plenty of very useful introductory articles and guides from reputable web sites such as *The National Archives* and the *British Library*. Newspapers that are still in print often have a history of the newspaper available on their website.

Reviewing the on-line material is a good way to discover this topic. It will enable a general reader to identify the aspects that they would like to study in more detail and to check what is currently available in print or which library holds a copy.

Texts about newspaper history range from academic studies about specific aspects of newspapers at a particular time, through to textbooks for journalists. There are also biographies of the press barons of the early twentieth century, the role of the press during wartime and some very old histories.

Some researchers may wish to develop practical skills in the following areas to enable them to collect and analyse historical data.

Statistics

Libraries and bookshops have books ranging from introductory texts, that cover very basic concepts, through to books that cover advanced statistical techniques. As individuals usually have a preferred learning style, browse a selection of titles to find a book that covers the topic at the appropriate level and whose approach is appealing.

Researchers who wish to use advanced statistical techniques to select a sample or check the statistical validity of their results will need to study inferential statistics for information about the formulas and how to apply them.

Spreadsheets

A similar point applies to developing the generic skills to use a spreadsheet with confidence, browse a selection of titles to find a book that covers the topic at the appropriate level and whose approach is appealing.

An alternative is to join a class to develop spreadsheet skills. These may be available in community venues. People who belong to an educational establishment may have access to in-house tuition as part of their studies.

Research Methodology

The internet has plenty of material related to research methodologies. Using this as a starting point will enable a researcher to decide how deeply they wish, or need, to explore the topic and to identify further reading that suits their preferred learning style.

Index